THE
Protector de Indios

THE
Protector de Indios
IN COLONIAL NEW MEXICO,
1659–1821

Charles R. Cutter

Published in cooperation with the
Historical Society of New Mexico

University of New Mexico Press
Albuquerque

Design by Milenda Nan Ok Lee

Library of Congress Cataloging-in-Publication Data

Cutter, Charles R., 1950–
The protector de indios in colonial New Mexico,
1659–1821.

Bibliography: p.
Includes index.
1. Indians of Mexico—Legal status, laws, etc.—
History. 2. Legal assistance to Indians—Mexico—
History. I. Historical Society of New Mexico. II. Title.
KGF2200.C88 1986   346.7201'3   86-7033
ISBN 0-8263-0905-4   347.20613
ISBN 0-8263-0906-2 (pbk.)

Library of Congress Catalogue Card Number 86-7033.
International Standard Book Number:
0-8263-0905-4 (cloth)
0-8263-0906-2 (paper)
First Edition

For Maryann, Francisco, and Casandra

For Mike Worthington,

With Best Wishes,

Charles Cullen

San Antonio
12 November 1992

Contents

Foreword

The Historical Society of New Mexico is pleased to co-sponsor with the University of New Mexico Press Charles R. Cutter's *The Protector de Indios in Colonial New Mexico* as the eleventh volume in the joint publication program between the Society and the Press. This book provides a rare glimpse into Native American sociopolitical life spanning about five centuries—from the distant era of conquistadores and Ferdinand and Isabella's claim to the New World to the enduring impact of Spain's presence here, particularly as glimpsed in the cultures of Indians and Hispanics in the Southwest today.

Law has always been the companion of empire. However, colonial authorities often failed to uphold well-intentioned legislation. Spain, unlike other colonial powers, wrestled mightily with moral and legal questions about the provision for justice in their colonies. The *protector*, who was appointed by the Spanish government, represented the legal rights and privileges of the Indians. The *protector* was important as a means of providing access to the Spanish legal system, especially in colonial New Mexico. The role of the *protector de indios* remains a part of Pueblo Indian legacy to this very day, for it helped to establish precedents that are crucial to the native peoples' ability to protect their territorial privileges.

Cutter's book provides a detailed yet exciting study of not only the social and political ambiance involved in enforcing colonial law in the Indies but also how Spain, unlike no other European power, successfully exerted jurisdiction over the relations betwen Indians and colonists.

The author should be applauded for his skillful interpretation of historical facts, which makes his book a fine piece of literature apart from its scholarly value. The publication of this book adds another dimension to the ongoing debate between Indian and Hispanic groups over land rights. As with the other books in the copublication series, this one fulfills the Historical Society's and the University of New Mexico Press's hopes of creating interest, appreciation, and knowledge of the culture of the Southwest and reiterates the importance of history as a study in cultural change and adaptation.

The author, Charles R. Cutter, was a Fulbright scholar in Spain in 1985–86 and has done extensive studies and research on the country. He is a doctoral candidate in history at the University of New Mexico.

Acknowledgments

Many individuals have contributed in various ways to the realization of this work. I owe much to teachers, friends, and fellow students. In particular I wish to thank Richard Etulain, Gerald Nash, Ferenc Szasz, and Margaret Connell Szasz for their valuable comments at various stages of the manuscript. William Tydeman, and the entire staff at Special Collections, University of New Mexico Library, have been friendly and helpful.

To those scholars of Spanish Colonial history who have provided direction I am grateful. Frequent discussions with Peter Bakewell and John Kessell have been most stimulating and enlightening. Joseph Sanchez and Marc Simmons steered me to several pertinent documents. Myra Ellen Jenkins generously shared her learned opinions on various aspects of New Mexico's past.

Special thanks is due Richard Ellis for his guidance throughout my graduate studies. At UNM Press, David Holtby's careful eye and his personal interest in this work have greatly eased the editorial process. I thank all for their time and expertise. In the end, however, every author must assume responsibility for his output. Any errors of interpretation or muddled passages are my own.

Finally, my parents, my wife, and my children have always given me the love and encouragement that has made life satisfying as a historian.

Charles R. Cutter

Introduction

On 26 September 1816, five Indian men stood outside the thick stone walls of the *Real Audiencia* in Mexico City. Momentarily, they would appear before the secretary of the *Juzgado General de Indios* (General Indian Court), Don Francisco de Arteaga, to make arrangements for continuing their pending lawsuit *in absentia* before returning home. In the busy street, only a few blocks from the metropolitan center, Antonio Quintana, Santiago Coris, Manuel, Domingo, and Francisco probably reviewed last-minute courtroom strategy. Or perhaps they reflected upon the chain of events that had led them to the capital of New Spain. From the foyer, a court aide summoned the five men and they anxiously followed the *portero* to the secretary's chambers.

This was not an unusual scene. The Juzgado General de Indios, designed specifically for Indian litigation, heard numerous requests, complaints, and testimony, week in and week out. What was unusual, however, was that the five men did not live in Mexico City, or even in the great valley of Mexico. Antonio Quintana and his friends were natives of the Pueblo de Cochití. This community of Keresan people, located on the banks of the Río del Norte in the far northern province of Nuevo México, lay some seventeen hundred miles from the capital of New Spain. Confident of their rights as Indians, these men had made the long journey to Mexico City to personally present their side of a land dispute that had dragged on for years at the local level.

Like natives in other parts of the Spanish empire, the Pueblo Indians of New Mexico found in the Hispanic legal system a relatively effective means of resolving conflicts. Among the many offices and institutions designed to facilitate Indian participation in the judicial process was that of the *protector de indios,* the protector of Indians. Although other legal channels were available to Indians, the protector often played a major role in aiding them in judicial matters. Indeed, the activity of protectors at three jurisdictional levels contributed to a decision that favored the Pueblo de Cochití in this case.

This brief study examines the important role of the protector de indios in colonial New Mexico from 1659 to 1821. Of all the components of the Spanish legal system, the protector perhaps best embodies Spain's commitment to uphold Indian rights. His duty was to "aid and defend" the American natives and he did so, with varying degrees of success, throughout the course of Spanish rule. The office of protector de indios represents perhaps the highest expression of Spanish idealism in the treatment of natives of the New World.

Some may claim that Spanish law never provided true equity for Indians because it was based on European, not native, notions of justice. While not without some grain of truth, this argument nevertheless reflects the outlook of twentieth-century cultural pluralism. Provision for justice and equity in any historical period must be judged on its own terms. The extensive use that Indians made of Spanish legal machinery, including the protector, suggests that it must have functioned reasonably well. Spanish justice afforded at least a tolerable degree of legal protection for the Indians of New Mexico.

Historians and others have placed considerable emphasis upon the violent means by which colonial powers often forced Indians to adopt European modes of behavior. A much more subtle way of doing so was to superimpose the Spanish crown as the font of justice, and to provide readily accessible avenues to its legal system, thereby encouraging conflict resolution via Spanish institutions. The protector de indios represented one such important avenue, acting chiefly as a legal representative of the Indians in court. He had no authority over them, however, and, especially after the sixteenth century, usually acted only upon request of the natives. His role, then, was unlike that of the familiar Indian agent of Anglo-American history.

Neither of the other two major contemporary colonial powers, England or France, had a comparable official. Under those regimes Indians had little or no access to the respective colonial legal machinery.[1] Moreover, when In-

---

1. Alden T. Vaughan, *New England Frontier: Puritans and Indians, 1620–1675*, rev. ed. (New York and London: W. W. Norton and Company, 1979). Vaughan, the scholar perhaps most sympathetic to Puritan dealings with Indians, argues that before King Philip's War (1675–76), Indians in New England received equitable treatment under Puritan law. After the conflict, however, Indian participation in all aspects of Puritan life, including the legal system, dwindled. Likewise, Wilcomb E. Washburn, in *Red Man's Land/White Man's Law: A Study of the Past and Present Status of the American Indian* (New York:

dians did appear in English or French courts, they usually did so as passive participants, rather than initiators of litigation. This denial of use of the judicial system to Indians continued in Anglo-American practice after the American Revolution. Not until the twentieth century did native Americans effectively pursue justice through the court system of the United States. Thus, in a curious way, Spanish jurisprudence in colonial New Mexico presaged modern Indian use of this nation's legal machinery. As an important agent of the Spanish legal structure, the office of protector de indios in New Mexico merits attention.

Charles Scribner's Sons, 1971), pp. 44–45, views King Philip's War as a turning point in attempts to incorporate Indians into the New England political structure. A useful study of French policy is Cornelius J. Jaenen, *Friend and Foe: Aspects of French-Amerindian Cultural Contact in the Sixteenth and Seventeenth Centuries* (New York: Columbia University Press, 1976). Jaenen, in dispelling the traditional view of intercultural understanding between French and Indians, claims that the two cultures did not clash principally "because they remained largely isolated and separated from each other" (p. 194).

I

Genesis
and
Development

On the eve of New World discovery, Spain was perhaps the most legal-minded nation in Europe. Under the guidance of Fernando and Isabel, the Reyes Católicos, the newly united country had experienced a tremendous growth in institutions normally associated with the modern state.[1] One solid base of this modernization process was a firmly established legal tradition. Indeed, in the eyes of contemporary theorists, the prime function of monarchy was to provide legal justice. As might be expected, Spain attempted to transfer intact to the New World as much of her institutional structure as possible. Institutions based on peninsular experiences, however, required varying degrees of modification to conditions in the Americas. By far the most vexing problem that Spain faced centered on the status of indig-

---

1. For a succinct discussion of the early development of the modern Spanish state, see J. H. Elliot, *Imperial Spain, 1469–1716* (New York: New American Library, 1966), pp. 75–127.

enous peoples encountered on voyages of exploration. How were the American natives to be considered? What was the moral nature of these "primitive" peoples? Were they to fit into the fabric of society? And, if so, in what ways? Throughout much of the sixteenth century, Spanish jurists, theologians, and statesmen wrestled with these questions.[2]

Before long, Spain adopted the position that Indians were indeed capable of incorporation into Spanish life. Their perceived condition as "poor and wretched" people (*pobres y miserables*), however, excluded the natives from immediate and full-fledged citizenship. In the eyes of the law, therefore, they were considered as minors. This perception of Indians as legal minors continued until just before the end of Spanish control in America.[3] Although subordinate members, the American natives were to play a large role in colonial society, and Spain made a concerted effort to incorporate Indians into its economic, political, and religious systems. Throughout the colonial experience, then, the essence of Spanish policy for sedentary natives was that of inclusion, rather than exclusion.

2. On the debate over the status of Indians, see Lewis Hanke, *All Mankind Is One: A Study of the Disputation Between Bartolomé de Las Casas and Juan Ginés de Sepúlveda in 1550 on the Intellectual and Religious Capacity of American Indians* (DeKalb, Ill.: Northern Illinois University Press, 1974). An excellent brief study of Spanish notions of sovereignty is J. H. Parry, *The Spanish Theory of Empire in the Sixteenth Century* (New York: Octagon Books, 1974).

3. New Mexico State Archives and Records Center, Spanish Archives of New Mexico, 1621–1821 (hereafter cited as SANM II):673, "Causa Criminal contra las reas M.ª Franᶜᵃ y M.ª su madre sentenciadas a muerte con parecer de asesor," 22 April 1773. Similarly, documentation found in the Archivo de Hidalgo de Parral, Chihuahua, Mexico, from the seventeenth and eighteenth centuries confirms this legal status of Indians; see also José María Ots Capdequí, *Historia del Derecho Español en América y del Derecho Indiano* (Madrid: Aguilar, 1969), pp. 205–6.

Incorporation, of course, carried with it the responsibilities of protection. Given the prevailing organic view of society, theorists agreed that even the most humble "members" of the "body" were crucial to the well-being of the whole, and therefore were worthy of royal attention. The Indians, said one jurist, were the "feet which sustain and carry the weight of the entire body . . . of the Republic." Care had to be taken to "remove any obstacles which might cause a fall" and "injure the head" [that is, the crown].[4] In various ways, the crown sought to protect the "feet" of its colonial enterprise. Furthermore, Catholic idealism as well as sheer expediency compelled Spain to include native peoples within the "body" of her vast empire. While nearly every official in the colonial administrative network had the duty of watching out for Indian interests, the crown chose to create a position specifically for this task—the protector de indios.

Long before Spaniards arrived in the New World, the seeds of the office of protector de indios had been sown on the Iberian peninsula. During the Middle Ages, Spain had developed a sociolegal system that provided for the protection of those incapable of defending themselves. Pedro II of Aragón (1196–1213), for example, founded the office of *padre de huérfanos*, which had as its duties the tutelage and upbringing of orphaned children. Known in other parts of the Iberian peninsula as *padre de menores* and as *protector de huérfanos y niños pobres*, this municipal office continued in operation throughout the early modern period of Spanish

4. Juan de Solórzano Pereira, *Política Indiana* (Madrid: 1647; reprint, Madrid and Buenos Aires: Compañía Ibero-Americana de Publicaciones, S.A., 1930), libro 2, capítulo 28, números 21, 22.

history and was among the cultural baggage that Spain carried to the Americas.[5]

Similarly, a study of *Las Siete Partidas* of Alfonso X *el sabio* shows that the notion of protection for children was a firmly established precept of medieval Castilian law. Completed in 1265, the *Partidas* represent one of the great juridical accomplishments of the medieval world and has been considered the basis of Castilian law since the middle of the fourteenth century.[6] The laws of Castile governed Spanish possessions in the New World, and consequently the *Partidas* came to occupy a place of eminence in the courts of Spanish America, perhaps even more so than in Spain, where municipal and regional *fueros* (privileges) often conflicted.[7] A number of provisions in this monumental compilation, which touched upon almost every imaginable aspect of medieval life, contained the philosophical underpinnings upon which the office of protector de indios rested. Carefully regulated codes, for example, defined the conduct between orphans or minors and their guardians, tutors, and

5. Constantino Bayle, *El Protector de Indios* (Sevilla: Escuela de Estudios Hispano-Americanos de la Universidad de Sevilla, 1945), p. 5. Evidence of persistence of these offices on the peninsula is found in Manuela Fernández-Arroyo y Cabeza de Vaca and Jesús Villalmanzo Cameno, *Catálogo de la Serie de Real Justicia* (Madrid: Servicio de Publicaciones del Ministerio de Educación y Ciencias, 1976), p. 120; and José Simón Díaz, *Fuentes para la Historia de Madrid y su Provincia*, tomo 1 (Madrid: Instituto de Estudios Madrileños, 1964), p. 142.

6. John Thomas Vance, *The Background of Hispanic-American Law* (Washington, D.C.: Catholic University of America, 1937), provides useful historical summaries of the major bodies of Spanish legislation. For a discussion of the development and role of the *Partidas* in medieval Spain, see Marie R. Madden, *Political Theory and Law in Medieval Spain* (New York: Fordham University Press, 1930), pp. 65–97.

7. Ots Capdequí, *Historia del Derecho Español*, pp. 45–46.

curators (*curadores*). Particularly in matters of legal representation, obligations of the later protectors are evident in the *Partidas*. Indeed, so analogous, in Spanish eyes, was the relationship between the crown and its *niños con barba* (children with beards), that some jurists specifically likened the role of the protector to that of the tutor.[8] The first official appointee to the office of protector de indios was the champion of the natives during a long series of sixteenth-century debates, the Dominican Fray Bartolomé de Las Casas.[9] Las Casas arrived in the Caribbean in 1502 and a decade later received a share of an encomienda on the island of Cuba. After witnessing the destructive effects of that institution, however, he renounced his title as an encomendero and began a lifelong crusade against the encomienda and in defense of the Indians.[10] Returning to Spain in 1515 to plead the case of the natives, Las Casas managed to gain an audience with the aging monarch, Fernando *el Católico*, now a widower, who had previously shown little pity for indigenous Americans. When the king died shortly thereafter, Las Casas found the sympathetic ear of the regent Cardinal Francisco Jiménez de Cisneros, perhaps the greatest Spanish statesman of the age. The

8. *Las Siete Partidas del Sabio Rey don Alonso el nono* (Salamanca: Andrea de Portonaris, 1555; facsimile reprint, Madrid: Boletín Oficial del Estado, 1974). See, for example, ley 5, título 11, partida 3; and l. 7, tít. 2, part. 3.; Solórzano Pereira, *Política Indiana*, lib. 2, cap. 28, núm. 51.

9. On the life of Bartolomé de Las Casas, and his significance to the development of Spanish Indian policy, see Lewis Hanke, *The Spanish Struggle for Justice in the Conquest of America* (Philadelphia: University of Pennsylvania Press, 1949). Also useful is Henry Raup Wagner, with the collaboration of Helen Rand Parish, *The Life and Writings of Bartolomé de las Casas* (Albuquerque: University of New Mexico Press, 1967).

10. C. H. Haring, *The Spanish Empire in America* (New York: Oxford University Press, 1947), pp. 44–45.

persistent Dominican presented his proposals for ending the mistreatment of the Indians and for establishing a humane system of governing the colonies. Impressed, Cisneros appointed a council to deliberate on the appropriate action to be taken.[11]

Under the influence of Las Casas, the council recommended, among other things, the suppression of all encomiendas, separation of Spanish towns from native towns, freedom for the Indians, and clerical administration of the colony. Cardinal Cisneros demonstrated his sympathy for the plight of the natives by accepting the program and placing the Order of St. Jerome in charge of carrying out the proposals of the council. Although Las Casas was not to be one of the administrators, he did have first choice in selecting the candidates who were to sail to Española and administer that colony.

Before the group left the peninsula, however, differences arose between the Jeronimites and Las Casas. The idealistic Dominican demanded that Cisneros appoint another set of administrators who would be more pliable to his will. This the regent refused to do. But he did bestow upon Las Casas the sonorous, if somewhat ambiguous, title of "universal protector of all the Indians of the Indies," and in 1516 sent him back to America to watch after and report on native affairs.[12] Ultimately, the attempt to establish clerical au-

---

11. Lesley Byrd Simpson, *The Encomienda in New Spain: The Beginning of Spanish Mexico* (Berkeley and Los Angeles: University of California Press, 1966), pp. 39–41.

12. Néstor Meza Villalobos, *Historia de la Política Indígena del Estado Español en América* (Santiago: Ediciones de la Universidad de Chile, 1976), pp. 47–52; Simpson, *Encomienda*, p. 40; Hanke, *Spanish Struggle for Justice*, p. 42; Haring, *Spanish Empire*, p. 45; Bartolomé de Las Casas, *Historia de las Indias* (México and Buenos Aires: Fondo de Cultura Económica, 1951), libro 3,

thority in the colonies failed, but the first major step for protecting the Indians had been taken. Furthermore, a precedent had been set—the clergy first assumed the role of official protectores de indios. As colonization extended from the Antilles to the mainland, Spain generally adopted the practice of appointing regional prelates as protectors of the natives. In colonies where there was no bishop, other clerics were given charge of the position.[13] With the powers of the new office as yet ill-defined, these early protectors often took considerable latitude in enforcing royal orders relative to Indian treatment.[14]

In Mexico, Archbishop Juan de Zumárraga interpreted the powers of protectorship quite broadly, and he soon found himself in conflict with the members of the Audiencia of New Spain. At one level, Zumárraga sought to curb illegal exploitation of the natives by audiencia officials, but a more important struggle revolved around questions of authority and jurisdiction in regulating Spanish–Indian relations.[15] Las Casas's role as protector had been that of an adviser on Indian affairs, a "conscience" of the crown. Zumárraga be-

---

capítulo 90. Edición de Agustín Millares Carlo y estudio preliminar de Lewis Hanke. Most of the previously cited historians rely heavily on Las Casas for the early history of Spanish–Indian relations.

13. Enrique Otte, *Cédulas Reales Relativas a Venezuela, 1500–1550* (Caracas: Fundación John Boulton y La Fundación Eugenio Mendoza, 1963), p. 284; Meza, *Historia de la Política Indígena*, pp. 162–63; Bayle, *Protector de Indios*, p. 34.

14. For an example of the crown's instructions to these prelate protectors, see Vasco de Puga, *Provisiones, Cédulas, Instrucciones Para el Gobierno de la Nueva España* (México: Pedro Ocharte, 1563; facsimile reprint, Madrid: Ediciones Cultura Hispánica, 1945), folio 64; Meza, *Historia de la Política Indígena*, pp. 162–63.

15. Silvio Zavala, *La Encomienda Indiana*, segunda edición (México: Editorial Porrúa, S.A., 1973), p. 345.

lieved that the office carried with it the power to enforce protective legislation. Fearing a rival, the *oidores* (judges) of the audiencia at first refused to recognize Zumárraga's appointment on the pretext that the prelate had set sail for America before his commission as archbishop had been confirmed. They then proceeded to hinder his actions on behalf of the Indians.

Mexico became the scene of a struggle between civil and clerical authority, as both sides sought to gain the upper hand. Writing to the emperor in July 1529, the audiencia members requested that they alone have the right to visit and protect the natives of the country. Zumárraga countered with a scathing denunciation of the audiencia to the emperor and asked that the office of protector be invested with even greater powers.[16]

As a result of this heated controversy between Zumárraga and the audiencia, the crown sought to define more clearly the nature of the position in order to avoid a destructive confrontation between the civil and clerical arms of government. A royal *cédula*, dated 2 August 1530, further clarified the role of protector de indios. The decree stipulated that the protector could send representatives to areas within his ecclesiastical jurisdiction to look after the well-being of natives, but that these officials had to have the audiencia's prior approval. Second, the protector, or his representatives, could conduct investigations into Spanish mistreatment of Indians, but must send the information to the president and oidores of the audiencia for deliberation. In

16. Joaquín García Icazbalceta, *Don Fray Juan de Zumárraga, Primer Obispo y Arzobispo de Mexico,* vol. 1 (México: Editorial Porrúa, S.A., 1947), pp. 49–65; Zavala, *Encomienda Indiana,* pp. 344–45; Simpson, *Encomienda,* appendix 3, pp. 214–29.

cases where misconduct warranted punishment, the protector might impose a fine of up to fifty gold pesos, or a sentence of up to ten days in jail with no possible appeal. For any fine over these limits, the convicted person had the right to appeal the sentence to the audiencia. Finally, the protector, and those acting in his name, could go to any part of the province to gain information concerning the misconduct of any Spaniard toward Indians. Even the conduct of royal officials, such as *corregidores* and *alguaciles*, might come under investigation. But, emphasized the cédula, "it is not our intention or purpose that the protectors have any superiority over said magistrates."[17]

Quite clearly, these instructions, and particularly this last clause, weakened the powers of the protector de indios as Zumárraga perceived them. Responding realistically, and insisting upon royal prerogative, the crown demonstrated that it would not relinquish its New World acquisitions to idealistic churchmen imbued with apostolic zeal. No millennial kingdom on earth would be established.[18] In the strange mixture that constituted Spanish colonialism, elements of economic enterprise and military conquest were too strong to let such a utopian vision take root in New Spain. Zumárraga's attempt to make civil authority subject to clerical will, however benevolent it may have seemed, was plainly not in accord with the ruling bodies in Spain.

Although the duties of office had been defined somewhat, the mid-sixteenth century still reflected considerable am-

---

17. Puga, *Provisiones*, f. 65.
18. Throughout the sixteenth century, however, the establishment of a Christian utopia of this type remained the goal of many influential clergymen. See John Leddy Phelan, *The Millennial Kingdom of the Franciscans in the New World*, 2d ed. (Berkeley and Los Angeles: University of California Press, 1970).

biguity over the nature of protectorship. In 1539, the protector of the Indians of Guatemala, Bishop Francisco Marroquín, wrote to the emperor of the

necessity that Your Majesty declare what it is to be a protector, and what it includes, and if we are judges, and if as such we might name alguaciles and notaries (*escribanos*) to execute our commands, and if the visitors we send may carry staffs of office (*varas*) since they go as judges. . . . These people should have not one, but many protectors. I implore Your Majesty to decree clearly on each of these points so that differences between us and the governors may be ended.[19]

In addition to continued uncertainty of obligations, the office of protector de indios suffered from other problems during the mid-sixteenth century. First, the position was alternately abolished and reinstated in various areas of Spanish America. Second, protectorship was no longer strictly the domain of the clergy, and the ensuing struggle for control of the office often soured relations between the civil and religious authorities. In Nueva Granada, for example, the Audiencia of Santa Fé de Bogotá outmaneuvered the local bishop, Juan de los Barrios, and acquired from the crown the right to name a civilian as "protector e defensor de los indios."[20] The Audiencia of Nueva Galicia in New Spain, on the other hand, took up the duties of protection as a

19. Archivo Histórico Nacional, Madrid (hereafter cited as AHN), Diversos, Documentos de Indias 26, "Carta del obispo de guatemala al Rey," Santiago de Guatemala, 27 August 1539.

20. Enrique Ortega Ricaurte, *Acuerdos de la Real Audiencia del Nuevo Reino de Granada*, tomo 2 (Bogotá: Archivo Nacional de Colombia, 1948), pp. 45–46; María Ángeles Eugenio Martínez, *Tributo y Trabajo del Indio en Nueva Granada* (Sevilla: Escuela de Estudios Hispano-Americanos de Sevilla, 1977), pp. 530–31.

body without naming a specific individual to the position.[21] Moreover, many colonial jurisdictions employed officials to watch out for the interests of Indians engaged in specific activities. One such official carried the amazingly exact title of *"alguacil amparador* (constable protector) of the Indians who come to the city to sell fruit."[22] The crown apparently was content to let the civil arm of government take over the duties of protection that had previously been the responsibility of the clergy.

By the mid-sixteenth century, a clear shift toward civil control of Indian protection characterized royal policy. One reason for the rise of civilians as protectors was probably the increase of litigation among natives during the middle period. In many areas, especially among more sophisticated native cultures, Indians adapted readily to the Spanish legal system.[23] At the same time, changes in Spanish society reinforced this trend. On the peninsula, Castile was experiencing an era of tremendous growth in the influence of royal courts of law and a corresponding dependence upon

21. *Colección de Documentos Inéditos de Ultramar,* tomo 22 (Madrid: 1885–1932), p. 12, "De los visitadores de los indios, jueces, defensores, administradores y protectores de ellos," núm. 26 (August 1552).
22. Alfonso Caso et al., *Métodos y Resultados de la Política Indigenista en México* (México: Instituto Nacional Indigenista, 1954), p. 62.
23. Steve J. Stern, *Peru's Indian Peoples and the Challenge of Spanish Conquest: Huamanga to 1640* (Madison: University of Wisconsin Press, 1982), pp. 114–37, aptly demonstrates effective native use of Spanish legal mechanisms to uphold recognized land rights and work quotas in colonial Peru; see also William B. Taylor, *Landlord and Peasant in Colonial Oaxaca* (Stanford, Calif.: Stanford University Press, 1972), pp. 82–110; Charles Gibson, *Tlaxcala in the Sixteenth Century* (Stanford, Calif.: Stanford University Press, 1967), p. 77. In a recent study, Jerome A. Offner, *Law and Politics in Aztec Texcoco* (Cambridge: Cambridge University Press, 1984), points out that Texcocan legal culture was fairly sophisticated and well conceived even prior to European contact.

litigation as a means of resolving conflicts.[24] As a result, the legal profession flourished in contemporary Spain. In the Americas, this growth manifested itself in a proliferation of attorneys, known as *abogados de indios* and *procuradores de indios*, who catered to the brisk business of representing Indians in litigation. These self-appointed protectors made their living off the natives. Given the climate of the times, the emergence of civilian protectors schooled in law may have been welcomed as the best way to defend native rights. A specialist of this type might satisfy the needs of Indian and Spaniard alike more effectively than the clergy, who relied chiefly on the weight of moral suasion.

Although the crown had taken tentative steps in 1554 to divest the clergy of official protectorship by giving the Audiencia of New Spain charge of litigation involving poor Indians, more decisive action came nine years later. In a cédula of 6 September 1563, *fiscales* (royal attorneys) of the New World audiencias acquired the function of protector and were instructed to act on behalf of the natives in "things in which they should be defended and aided, in general as well as in particular."[25]

With this action the office came dangerously close to extinction as a separate entity. Abuses stemming from lack of royal control over the protectorship contributed to its near demise. One astute contemporary, Viceroy Francisco de Toledo, observed that many self-appointed protectors

24. Richard L. Kagan, *Lawsuits and Litigants in Castile: 1500–1700* (Chapel Hill: University of North Carolina Press, 1981), pp. 137–62. This book is an excellent study of contemporary Castilian legal practice.

25. Diego de Encinas, *Cedulario Indiano* (Madrid: Imprenta Real, 1596; facsimile reprint, Madrid: Ediciones Cultura Hispánica, 1945), libro 2, folio 270; lib. 2, ff. 268–69.

and defensores were more than willing to defend the Indians from others, but took advantage of the natives themselves.[26] Indians often paid fees far out of proportion to the legal services rendered.[27] Consequently, in 1567 the crown outlawed the positions of protector, defensor, and *promotor de indios* (all were legal representatives of some sort) in the jurisdiction served by the Audiencia of Quito.[28] Earlier royal policy had displayed an increasing reluctance to appoint clergymen as protectores de indios. The crown now seemed unwilling to assign the responsibility of Indian protection to any single office.

Despite shifting royal policy, American natives continued to use the Spanish legal system, and to employ legal counsel, in settling disputes. Especially in Peru and Mexico, Indians often spent considerable time and money in pursuing both communal and individual litigation. Colonial authorities repeatedly expressed concern that the courts were becoming bogged down by an endless stream of petty disputes. Even more disquieting was the frequency with which natives abandoned their lands and traveled great distances to obtain royal justice.[29] Aside from considerations of the physical hardships, colonial officials realized that these lengthy journeys hindered effective political administration and tribute collection. To remedy these and other problems, Viceroy

26. *Colección de Documentos Inéditos para la Historia de España*, tomo 94 (Madrid: 1842–1895) (hereafter cited as *D.I.E.*), pp. 296–97, "Relación sumaria de lo que el Virrey don Francisco de Toledo escribió en lo tocante al gobierno espiritual, y temporal, y guerra, y hacienda."
27. Solórzano Pereira, *Política Indiana*, lib. 2, cap. 28, núm. 48.
28. Encinas, *Cedulario Indiano*, lib. 4, f. 333.
29. Biblioteca Nacional, Madrid (hereafter cited as BNM) MS 2927, "Cédulas y Provisiones para el Reino de Perú," f. 174; *D.I.E.*, tomo 94, pp. 282–83, "Relación sumaria . . . [del] Virrey don Francisco de Toledo."

Chapter 1

Francisco de Toledo (1569–81) issued in 1575 a set of twenty-two ordinances that established guidelines for defensores de indios. The precedents set in his *ordenanzas* formed the basis of the office of protector de indios in its final form and left their imprint on the position throughout the empire.[30] Toledo established strict government control over the appointment of protectors, not only at a superior level for the audiencia, but also at a local level in "every Spanish city of this kingdom," in order to eliminate self-appointed defensores. To ensure a higher degree of honesty, ordinances fixed the protectors' salaries at an adequate sum and prohibited them from accepting any gratuities.[31] Finally, Toledo detailed more explicitly than before the obligations of the protector. Among their most important duties were those of safeguarding communal lands, reporting illegal working conditions, and seeing that all legislation favoring the natives was obeyed.[32]

Despite these and other measures, Viceroy Toledo had his enemies, and many of his reforms met with opposition in the colonies and at court. Moreover, abuses of the office of protector de indios continued in various parts of the empire. In a cédula dated 27 May 1582, the crown resolved

30. The most complete work concerning the activity of Toledo is Roberto Levillier, *Don Francisco de Toledo: Supremo Organizador del Perú: Su Vida, Su Obra (1515–1582)* (Madrid: Espasa-Calpe, S.A., 1935).

31. *Recopilación de Leyes de Los Reynos de Las Indias* (Madrid: Julián de Paredes, 1681; facsimile reprint, Madrid: Ediciones Cultura Hispánica, 1973), l. 2, tít. 6, lib. 6; Bayle, *Protector de Indios*, p. 88.

32. Roberto Levillier, *Gobernantes del Perú: Cartas y Papeles, Siglo XVI*, tomo 8 (Madrid: Biblioteca del Congreso Argentino, 1925), pp. 281–98, "Ordenanzas del Virrey Don Francisco de Toledo, relativas al defensor general de los naturales." Arequipa, 10 September 1575.

to definitively terminate the position. The fiscales of the audiencias were instructed to aid all natives (not just the poor) in legal matters.[33] Again, however, the need for a full-time legal representative for the Indians became obvious. Natives continued to use the Spanish legal system to settle their differences. Having no protectores, they now spent "vast amounts of silver pesos which they took from their community chests, and wasted on secretaries, notaries, lawyers, procuradores, and defensores" who took advantage of the Indians' willingness to pay hefty retainers. As a result, Philip II issued another cédula, dated 10 January 1589, that formally reestablished the office of protector de indios.[34] Borrowing heavily from Toledo's regulations, the crown took the final step in making the position a strictly civil function under theoretically tight government control. The office retained its essential features throughout the colonial period until 1821, when it was again abolished in the wake of early nineteenth-century liberal reform.[35]

As with so many other Spanish colonial institutions, the sixteenth century proved to be crucial in the formation of the office of protector de indios. During this early period, when Spain sought specific ways to provide for Indian protection, three discernible phases marked the evolution of the office. Initially, prelate protectors held judicial powers as well as the authority to execute their decisions. The resulting clash between civilians and clergy, and royal efforts to restore harmony, led to the crown's fateful decision to

---

33. BNM, MS 2927, "Cédulas y Provisiones para el Reino de Perú," f. 166v.; Encinas, *Cedulario Indiano*, lib. 4, f. 333.
34. Encinas, *Cedulario Indiano*, lib. 4, f. 334.
35. The decree abolishing the office is found in AHN, Reales Cédulas 4.990.

diminish the protector's role to an advisory capacity. During the middle period, another change, more subtle but no less significant, saw civil officials emerge as competitors for the office. While this transition no doubt reflected the growing influence of the legal profession in contemporary Spanish society, it likewise underscored the Indians' increasing dependence on Spanish legal machinery for resolving conflicts.

The final phase of development saw the establishment of civilian control of the office, the principal duties of which were as a legal representative of the Indians. Although the clergy still had a responsibility to protect the Indians, they lacked the official title. By the last decade of the sixteenth century, the crown had painfully worked out its concepts of, and solutions for, Indian protection. Theoretical debate over the nature of the colonial enterprise faded into the background. The time had come for implementation of practical programs that facilitated effective administration. In its transformation from an idealistic position to a more pragmatic one, the office of protector de indios embodies the direction of Spanish colonial policy as colonists on the frontier of New Spain prepared to push northward to *"la nueva México."*[36]

36. "La nueva México" was common usage in colonial New Mexico. Mexico refers here to the city not the geographic region of today. Therefore, "nueva" is the implied modifier of "ciudad," a feminine noun.

2

The Protector
in Early New Mexico

When the adventurers of the Coronado expedition (1540–42) first entered the area now known as New Mexico, they were no doubt more disillusioned than impressed with Pueblo Indian culture. No dazzling city, no "other Mexico" awaited them. Instead, they found villages of adobe and stone. In spite of their disappointment, the Spaniards recognized that the Indians who inhabited the Rio Grande Valley and its periphery were by far the most advanced peoples they had seen since pushing beyond central Mexico. Indeed, a chronicler of the expedition, Pedro de Castañeda, noted that "the natives here are intelligent people . . . There is no drunkenness, sodomy, or human sacrifice among them," he continued, "nor do they eat human flesh, or steal." Castañeda also found worthy of comment their modesty in dress as well as the architectural sophistication and cleanliness of their villages.[1]

---

1. George P. Hammond and Agapito Rey, ed. and trans., *Narratives of the Coronado Expedition, 1540–1542* (Albuquerque: University of New Mexico Press, 1940), pp. 252–56.

Chapter 2

Prehistorically, Pueblo culture centered in the modern Four Corners area of Utah, Colorado, Arizona, and New Mexico. Settlement size varied greatly, but one characteristic of the precontact period, from 1100 to 1300 A.D., was the presence of a number of large population clusters. For example, Pueblo Bonito, located at Chaco Canyon in northwestern New Mexico, boasted some eight hundred rooms that were used for living quarters as well as for storage. These large towns also featured distinctive interior courtyards, or plazas, and great kivas that were crucial to ceremonial life. Chaco Canyon appears to have been a major trade center within a larger network that reached as far as central Mexico and the Pacific Ocean. Pueblo culture declined somewhat in the thirteenth century for a variety of reasons, including drought, erosion, and famine. In successive waves, the Pueblos left the Colorado Plateau and migrated to more stable water supplies.[2]

Spaniards found the Pueblos in their new location, situated primarily in the Rio Grande Valley, as well as in some outlying areas such as Pecos, Ácoma, Zuñi, and the Hopi villages. Like their predecessors, these new villages were relatively large in size and featured a plaza as the community center. While variation from village to village existed, common features afforded some degree of cultural unity. Irri-

2. Linda S. Cordell, "Prehistory: Eastern Anasazi," in Alfonso Ortiz, ed., *Handbook of North American Indians: The Southwest*, vol. 9 (Washington, D.C.: Smithsonian Institution, 1979), pp. 138–42. For more on Pueblo culture at the time of contact, see Edward P. Dozier, *The Pueblo Indians of North America* (New York: Holt, Rinehart and Winston, 1970); Alfonso Ortiz, ed., *Handbook of North American Indians: The Southwest*, vol. 9 (Washington, D.C.: Smithsonian Institution, 1979); and Edward H. Spicer, *Cycles of Conquest: The Impact of Spain, Mexico, and the United States on the Indians of the Southwest, 1533–1960* (Tucson: University of Arizona Press, 1962).

gated agriculture was the lifeblood of village economic activity, and the Pueblos seem to have possessed a clear sense of community boundaries. Seasonal hunting and gathering supplemented their crops of maize, beans, squash, and cotton. The extensive trade network continued to operate with vigor during this protohistoric period.[3] While well-built, multitiered adobe or stone dwellings were perhaps the most distinctive features of Pueblo technology, these natives were also accomplished weavers, potters, and jewelers. Another cohesive element of Pueblo life was the elaborate ceremonial religion headed by priesthoods.

If similarities among villages existed, however, so did important differences. The linguistic barriers between Pueblo groups served to reinforce the independence of the various communities. Authorities differ on exact designations, but Tiwa, Tewa, Towa, Keres, Tano, and Piro appear to have been the main groupings. Mutually unintelligible dialects within a number of these distinct languages further complicated inter-Pueblo communication. A more important divisive element than language was the staunch political autonomy of each pueblo. Normally, Pueblo leaders exercised no authority outside their respective villages. Shifting military alliances and regular warfare between Pueblo groups underscores the firmly embedded independence of each village.

The label *Pueblo,* then, conveys a picture of unity that simply did not exist among the sedentary natives of New Mexico. Spaniards referred to these people as *indios de pueblo,*

---

3. Carroll J. Riley, *The Frontier People: The Greater Southwest in the Protohistoric Period* (Carbondale, Ill.: Center for Archaeological Investigations, Southern Illinois University at Carbondale, 1982), pp. 119–21.

or "village Indians," in order to distinguish them from the nonsedentary *indios bárbaros*—such as the Apaches, Utes, and Comanches—who refused to live in fixed villages. Nonetheless, Spaniards consistently recognized linguistic and political differences between villages. Colonial documentation, for example, usually refers to individual Indians as "of the Keres nation," or "of the Indian pueblo of San Felipe." Thus, while Pueblo culture at the time of contact was sophisticated, it was not unified. But perhaps these traditions of internal cohesion and strong attachment to communal land were crucial in the Pueblos' subsequent ability to adapt to Spanish law as a method of preserving their physical and cultural identities.

Between the upper Rio Grande Valley and the rich Bajío of central Mexico lies an immense, high plateau that until recently was only sparsely populated. As Spanish expansion continued northward up the plateau of Mexico into the present-day area of Zacatecas–San Luis Potosí, the Europeans met stiff resistance from many small warlike nomadic bands of Indians who inhabited the region. Known generally as *chichimecas*, these fierce natives of northern New Spain did not recognize tribute systems, and refused to submit to Spanish authority as had their counterparts in central Mexico. Continual raids by the chichimecas made colonization difficult, but the discovery of rich silver strikes, and the promise of fabulous wealth, drew the adventurous northward. Raiding and retaliation escalated, and the two adversaries found themselves engulfed in an all-out confrontation, a *"guerra a fuego y a sangre,"* that lasted nearly forty years, from the late 1540s until well into the 1580s.

These hostilities hindered efficient exploitation of the region's tremendous mineral wealth. Military force alone had proved ineffective in pacifying the chichimecas who surrounded the silver-mining camps. Saddled with enormous fiscal burdens caused by imperial policy in Europe, the crown considered other alternatives to achieve peace with the chichimecas and thereby tap more effectively the resources of its colony. Finally, under the impetus of Viceroy Luis de Velasco II (1590–95), Spain adopted a new peace program to lure the chichimecas into permanent settlements.[4]

Using the concept of protection for settled natives as the cornerstone of the pacification program, Miguel de Caldera, the dynamic mestizo colonizer of the *gran chichimeca,* effectively implemented Spanish policy on the rugged northern frontier. Velasco appointed Caldera, a popular figure among the Indians, chief justice (*justicia mayor*) of the new settlements. The viceroy instructed him to protect and defend the natives against "injuries or mistreatment by any other persons, and proceed against any such persons who might treat these Indians in such a way as to cause them to rebel, punishing such persons as criminals."[5] The viceroy also commissioned several Spaniards, recommended by Caldera, as protectors of various chichimeca groups. In the volatile climate of the northern frontier, these men had more responsibility than that of simple legal representation.

Physical protection from marauding Indians and Spanish

4. Philip Wayne Powell, *Soldiers, Indians and Silver: The Northward Advance of New Spain, 1550–1600* (Berkeley and Los Angeles: University of California Press, 1952), is a useful account of the Spanish–Chichimeca clash on the northern frontier.

5. Quoted in Philip Wayne Powell, *Mexico's Miguel Caldera: The Taming of America's First Frontier, 1548–1597* (Tucson: University of Arizona Press, 1977), p. 134.

slavers was a critical duty in this frontier situation. Significantly, this official was often referred to as *capitán protector* (captain-protector), a title that aptly conveys the military importance of his obligations. As part of the plan to draw the nomadic natives into stable agricultural villages, the protector had the added task of overseeing distribution of food and clothing.[6]

Throughout the colonial period, the office of protector de indios continued to be an important one for the natives of those northern frontier areas settled at an early date. For example, the *alcalde mayor* of San Luis Potosí usually carried the additional title of protector of the chichimecas and *tlascaltecas*.[7] The fact that both the newly incorporated "wild" chichimecas and the staunchly loyal tlascaltecas (who were instrumental as cultural go-betweens in the Hispanicization of frontier Indians) received the benefits of a protector demonstrates the overarching unity of Spanish Indian policy. Records from the colonial archives of Parral, Chihuahua, indicate the persistence and importance of the position in the mining region of Saltillo and elsewhere. Representation in criminal proceedings and protection of property are just two examples of the protectors' activities.[8] Clearly, the protector played a major part in Spain's efforts to pacify and Hispanicize Indians in northern New Spain.

6. Powell, *Mexico's Miguel Caldera*, pp. 134–35; Archivo General de Indias (hereafter cited as AGI) Contaduría, ramo 10, "Cuenta de Vicente de Zaldívar desde 1593 a 1601"; ramo 2, "Certificación de la cuenta del Capitán Juan de Morlete," 1603.

7. Powell, *Soldiers, Indians and Silver*, pp. 280–81n. 34.

8. Archivo de Hidalgo de Parral (hereafter cited as AHP), r. 1635, fr. 796–810, "Caussa Criminal por querella dada por el Cap.ᵃⁿ diego Romo de bibar Contra gabriel yndio por ladrón," 14 April 1635; AHP r. 1680C, fr. 1550–57, "Criminal contra un Yndio llamado Lucas por abigeato," 12 January 1680.

The Protector in Early New Mexico

Once Spanish control of the rich silver mining areas was relatively secure, many colonists turned their attention northward to New Mexico, where they hoped to repeat the dizzying success of the Zacatecas strikes. The stable and sophisticated Pueblo groups only increased the attraction of the region. While contenders for the privilege of colonizing "la nueva México" maneuvered in New Spain's capital, several unauthorized expeditions made their way into the region in the last two decades of the sixteenth century.[9] It was in connection with the illegal *entrada* of Gaspar Castaño de Sosa, in 1590–91, that the protector de indios first appears in the annals of New Mexico history.

Although the purpose of Castaño's expedition is unclear, he probably intended to settle New Mexico and hoped for ex-post facto royal sanction of his efforts.[10] But Castaño also had been associated with those frontier Spaniards who engaged in profit-making slaving expeditions that partially supplied the labor force in some of the northern mines.[11] Spanish officials recognized this sort of slaving activity as a source of friction that hampered relations between natives

9. See George P. Hammond and Agapito Rey, *The Rediscovery of New Mexico, 1580–1594: The Explorations of Chamuscado, Espejo, Castaño de Sosa, Morlete, and Leyva de Bonilla and Humaña* (Albuquerque: University of New Mexico Press, 1966).
10. Albert H. Schroeder and Dan S. Matson, *A Colony on the Move: Gaspar Castaño de Sosa's Journal, 1590–1591* (Santa Fe: School of American Research, 1965), p. 5.
11. Powell, *Soldiers, Indians and Silver*, pp. 193–94; Robert C. West, *The Mining Community in Northern New Spain: The Parral Mining District* (Berkeley and Los Angeles: University of California Press, 1949), p. 52. Peter J. Bakewell, *Silver Mining and Society in Colonial Mexico: Zacatecas, 1546–1700* (Cambridge: Cambridge University Press, 1971), pp. 122–29, downplays the importance of Indian slave labor and stresses, instead, the wide use of free wage labor in and near Zacatecas.

and colonists, since slavers often failed to differentiate between peaceful and "rebellious" Indians.[12] Although often overlooked, the official sent to arrest Castaño was a highly regarded protector de indios, Juan Morlete.[13] The principal reason for Castaño's arrest is revealed in a contemporary source which noted that he had acted "without license from His Majesty."[14] But in light of Castaño's past activities, Morlete and his fifty companions may well have been trying to avert potential hostilities for colonists in the North. Philip II's Ordinances of Pacification of 1573 called for peaceful settlement only, and Castaño and company had certainly done nothing to calm the fears of New Mexico Indians. Indeed, many had fled to the mountains.[15] Removal of a troublemaker, then, fit the new frontier policy of peace and protection.

While unsanctioned occupation was not to be permitted, official interest in the northern frontier persisted. Royal approval for the colonization of New Mexico was granted to Juan de Oñate in 1595. Son of a millionaire Zacatecas miner, with impressive connections in both America and

12. See, for example, AGI México 69, Arteaga de Mendiola to King, México, 30 March 1596, in which Arteaga, the protector fiscal of the Audiencia of Mexico, complained about slavers on the northern frontier.

13. Powell, Mexico's Miguel Caldera, pp. 143, 247.

14. Colección de Documentos Inéditos Relativos al Descubrimiento, Conquista y Colonización de las Posesiones en América y Oceanía, tomo 15 (Madrid: 1864–84) (hereafter cited as D.I.I.), p. 58, "Asiento y Capitulaciones . . . con Joan Bautista de Lomas Colmenares . . . ," 15 February 1589. Recopilación de Leyes de Los Reynos de las Indias (Madrid: Julián de Paredes, 1681; facsimile reprint, Madrid: Ediciones Cultura Hispánica, 1973), l. 4, tít. 1, lib. 4, prohibited any new discoveries without royal authority.

15. Recopilación, l. 6, tít. 1, lib. 4; l. 10, tít. 1, lib. 4. AGI Patronato 22, ramo 10, "trozo de carta del capitán Morquete [sic] al Virrey D. Luis de Velasco," Río de las Naças, 16 September 1591.

Spain, Oñate hoped to make the New Mexico venture pay off as an economic enterprise. [16] In contrast to the chichimecas' attainments, the permanent settlements and advanced agricultural and architectural techniques of the Pueblo Indians seemed to augur the existence of "another Mexico" that might add to the wealth of Spain. The prospective colonizers did not miss the parallels. Oñate reflected this attitude when, upon persuading a number of native groups to swear allegiance to Spain, the Indians agreed to render

obedience and vassalage to the king Don Felipe, Our Lord, and become his subjects and vassals as had the kingdoms of Mexico, Tezcuco, Mechoacan, Tlaxcala, Guatemala, and others, by which they might live in peace and justice, protected from their enemies, in orderliness, and aided in trades, arts, agriculture, and livestock. [17]

While the reality of conquest in New Mexico meant at times the use of brutal military force, the theoretical basis for protection nevertheless had been established in the act of obedience. After the Indians swore allegiance, the Spanish promised to refrain from use of arms. In addition, they agreed to assume the role of defender against any indigenous enemies. Acknowledgment of Spanish rule also brought the benefits of European material culture. Finally, Indians were to live under Spanish institutions, and this meant, of course, access to the legal system. One cannot argue that the Indians were ever on equal terms with Spanish colonists in

16. George P. Hammond and Agapito Rey, *Don Juan de Oñate: Colonizer of New Mexico, 1595–1628*, 2 vols. (Albuquerque: University of New Mexico Press, 1953), is an effective presentation of primary source material.
17. AGI Patronato 22, ramo 13, ff. 60v.–61, "Primer obidienzia que dieron los yndios del nueuo mex^co . . . ," 7 July 1598.

America. Still, the ideal availability of royal law to all was important. It was so important, in fact, that it constituted one of the justifications for conquest. From the beginning, the theoretical right of the Indians to use Spanish legal institutions formed a part of the colonial experience in New Mexico. Implementation of that right, especially in the seventeenth century, was another matter. But imperfect as the actual execution may have been, the idea existed and was instrumental in shaping the pattern of relationships in colonial society.

If Oñate's entry into the province has been well chronicled, a paucity of documentation for much of the seventeenth century hinders an understanding of the early history of New Mexico. Much of the record generated in the province during this period, and housed in the government archives in Santa Fe, perished during the Pueblo Revolt of 1680. While several historians have made imaginative use of existing manuscripts in other collections, the results are limited in scope and probably present a distorted view of early New Mexico history.[18] Thus, a survey of the office of protector de indios in seventeenth-century New Mexico must be sketchy at best.

Juan Morlete was the first protector to enter the "kingdom" of New Mexico, but the identity of the first protector of New Mexico Indians remains a mystery. No protector de indios is mentioned in connection with Coronado's expe-

---

18. France V. Scholes, for example, used the records of the Inquisition to reconstruct and provide an interpretive framework for seventeenth-century New Mexico before the Pueblo Revolt. See his *Troublous Times in New Mexico, 1659–1670* (Albuquerque: University of New Mexico Press, 1942), or "Civil Government and Society in New Mexico in the Seventeenth Century," *New Mexico Historical Review* 10 (April 1935):71–111.

dition. In the 1540s the office was still in its formative stages, and had only taken root in those areas firmly under Spanish control. With the first sanctioned colonization at the end of the century, the office may have arrived in New Mexico. Certainly, Juan de Oñate had the authority as *adelantado* to establish all necessary offices for the proper functioning of civil government.[19] In emulating the prominent position of the protector on the chichimeca frontier, Oñate perhaps invested his alcaldes or other officials with the additional title of protector, or capitán protector, for the various Pueblo nations. No documentation, however, substantiates this possibility. Curiously, when writing to Viceroy Monterrey in 1601, Fray Juan de Escalona referred to himself as "prelate and protector . . . , sent to this land [New Mexico] to prevent evil and to seek what is good for God's children."[20] Although Escalona possibly was an officially appointed protector, a cleric holding the office at this late date appears to be anachronistic. He likely was alluding to his general obligation as a clergyman to watch out for native interests.[21]

The first real evidence of a protector for Indians in New Mexico does not appear until 1659, in the trial of a twenty-seven-year-old Hopi named Juan Zuñi.[22] During the admin-

19. Francisco Morales Padrón, *Teoría y Leyes de la Conquista* (Madrid: Ediciones Cultura Hispánica del Centro Ibero-Americano de Cooperación, 1979), p. 503; *Recopilación*, l. 10, tít. 3, lib. 4. See also the terms of Oñate's contract in Hammond and Rey, *Don Juan de Oñate*, vol. 1, pp. 42–57.

20. Hammond and Rey, *Don Juan de Oñate*, vol. 2, p. 692.

21. *Recopilación*, l. 1, tít. 1, lib. 6; l. 14, tít. 6, lib. 6.

22. Scholes, *Troublous Times*, pp. 13–15; University of New Mexico General Library, Special Collections, photostat collection of Archivo General de la Nación, México (hereafter cited as UNMSC, AGN), Tierras, 3286, ff. 63v–71, "Autos hechos Y dem^{da}do De la R^l audiencia de Mex^{co} Por el S^{or} gen^l Don di° dioniçio de Peñalosa Vrizeño y Verdugo . . . ," 1662.

istration of Governor Juan de Samaniego y Jaca (1653–56), Juan Zuñi had been convicted of committing a sacrilegious impersonation of the village *guardián* Fray Alonso de Posada. In a judicial declaration, Juan admitted that he had summoned the Awatovi villagers to the church where, in the absence of Posada, he had mimicked for his audience several of the Catholic rites. As punishment for this sacrilege, and for "cohabiting with fourteen Indian women of said pueblo," Spanish authorities assigned him to the service of the *convento* (religious quarters) in Santa Fe. There he was to be instructed in the Christian faith.

Juan managed to gain further notoriety, continuing in his "depraved manner and with little fear of God [or] Royal Justice." Not only had he picked the lock and taken supplies from the convento storeroom, but authorities also found stolen dental instruments in his possession (*hierros de sacar muelas*). In February 1659, dismayed officials again charged Juan with theft, this time for having pilfered linens, sugar, chocolate, and other items from Juan de Mesta, who lived in the *casas reales* on the plaza. The Hopi and an Indian accomplice, Cristóbal Meco, had then sold the goods to a married couple who, in turn, resold them to residents of Santa Fe.[23]

In the subsequent trial of Juan and his cohort, Governor Juan Manso de Contreras (1656–59) ordered a protector de indios to appear on behalf of the men. Called upon to defend the Indians in the court proceedings, Captain Diego

---

23. The word *meco* was used in Mexico to mean "rude" or "savage," and was often applied to the *indios bárbaros* of the northern frontier. Thus, Meco may have been a descriptive designation rather than a proper name. See Francisco J. Santamaría, *Diccionario General de Americanismos* (México: Editorial Pedro Robredo, 1942).

Romero, "protector and defensor of the Christian natives," urged the governor to consider cultural differences in meting out his justice. The fact that they admitted their crimes with the same facility with which they had committed them, argued the protector, "must be attributed to their lack of judgment and their incompetence (*falta de juicio y poca capacidad*); indeed, among these natives being a thief . . . is not considered a crime." Diego Romero's accuracy in assessing cultural values is arguable, but he did possess a first-hand knowledge of indigenous ways. A native New Mexican, Romero was later brought before the Inquisition on charges of having taken part in a heathen marriage ritual.[24] But the protector's plea for absolving the defendants because of cultural differences did not sway Governor Manso. Both men received two hundred lashes in public. Juan drew an additional sentence of ten years forced labor, while Cristóbal Meco received five.

France V. Scholes notes that this is the only record of an Indian trial which has been preserved among the few remaining contemporary documents. Despite this observation, Scholes surprisingly asserts that the severe punishments imposed on the defendants were "doubtless typical" of many other trials of Indians during the period. On the contrary, the unusually harsh sentence was the reason that the trial came to light in the course of Manso's *residencia* (review of office).[25] The presence of a protector may reflect an established pattern of legal procedure in matters involving Indians, although one example is hardly conclusive

---

24. See John L. Kessell, "Diego Romero, the Plains Apaches, and the Inquisition," *The American West* 15 (May–June 1978):12–16.
25. UNMSC, AGN Tierras, 3286, ff. 59–60, "Autos . . . Peñalosa," 1662.

proof. How effectively the protector defended Indian rights during a relatively oppressive seventeenth-century Spanish regime is another matter.

The next reference to a protector de indios surfaces during the residencia of Governor Bernardo López de Mendizábal (1659–61). In the latter part of October 1661, Antonio González, second-generation New Mexican and *escribano* (notary) of the *cabildo* (municipal council) of Santa Fe, spoke on behalf of hundreds of Indians from throughout the province who had grievances against the ex-governor.[26] Virtually every pueblo in New Mexico had complaints to lodge, and most often, González represented an entire village. Generally, the charges were similar in form and content. Indians complained that López had not paid them for having carted *piñones*, salt, and firewood, or for having engaged in the production of such items as blankets, stockings (*medias*), and oxcarts. Following the allegations, the natives requested monetary compensation, often hundreds of pesos.

While usually representing entire Pueblo communities, the protector also spoke out on behalf of individual Indians who had complaints about López's conduct. Esteban Clemente, "governor of Salinas, Tagnos, and Pecos," was typical in his request for 169 pesos, 6 reales, for having made several trips to the Apaches of the Seven Rivers area to trade maize "and other items" for clothing. In another instance, a San Felipe woman named Juana demanded payment of two blankets to satisfy the ex-governor's debt for sixteen pairs of

---

26. All of the following charges against López are found in UNMSC, AGN Tierras 3268, leg. 2, "Petiçiones, y Papeles sueltos tocantes al Gen¹ Don Bernardo López de Mendizábal, y Don Diego de Peñalosa." Angelico Chavez, *Origins of New Mexico Families* (Santa Fe: Historical Society of New Mexico, 1954), p. 40.

stockings she had made for him. Similarly, an Apache woman asked to be reimbursed for needlepoint work. Still another woman charged the governor with having caused the death of her husband because he had been forced into service as a muleteer on a trip to Sonora and had died en route.[27] Although González represented an impressive number of natives, the results of his activity remain unclear; no surviving records indicate that the Indians were compensated. Furthermore, González's appointment as protector apparently was only for the purpose of carrying out the residencia. In the proceedings, he stated that he was "protector and defensor of the Christian natives of this kingdom, named by [incoming Governor Diego de Peñalosa] for the residencia . . . of Don Bernardo López de Mendizábal." In speaking for a prominent leader from Abó, Esteban Clemente, González asserted that he did so because Esteban "had no one to aid and defend him until now."[28] González's statements reveal the inconsistent application of the office of protector in New Mexico. Not only was the appointment of González temporary, but the natives evidently had no protector on a consistent basis.

Still another allusion to the existence of a protector de indios prior to the Pueblo Revolt dates from the early eighteenth century. In 1707, in an attempt to retain the governorship of the province, Francisco Cuervo y Valdés

27. A balanced general treatment of Indian women in this period is Cheryl J. Foote and Sandra K. Schackel, "Indian Women of New Mexico, 1535–1680," in Darlis A. Miller and Joan Jensen, ed., *New Mexico Women* (Albuquerque: University of New Mexico Press, 1986).
28. On the remarkable personage of Esteban Clemente, see John L. Kessell, "Esteban Clemente: Precursor of the Revolt," *El Palacio* 84 (Winter 1980–81):16–17.

summoned all the Pueblo leaders to Santa Fe to make a declaration of support for his activities as governor. At this meeting, the native caciques stated that this convocation of leaders was similar to those held forty years earlier during the administration of Governor Juan de Miranda (1664–65 and 1671–75) when the "caciques, governors, and captains . . . appeared before *sargento mayor* Francisco Gómez Robledo, their protector."[29] According to the calculations of the Indians, Gómez would have been protector in 1667, a date that roughly corresponds to Miranda's tenures as governor.

Although no other record of specific activity by Gómez as protector has surfaced, he probably was the protector during the period in question. From a prominent New Mexico family, Francisco Gómez Robledo played an active role in local affairs from midcentury to just after the reconquest of the lost province. He typifies the upper echelons of frontier society, so important in the second tier of colonial government, who often held this office in New Mexico.[30]

An important difference between the frontier and larger, more populated areas was in the training of those who carried the title of protector de indios. Protectors who sat in the regional audiencias often were jurists of considerable stature; even those at a provincial level in the heavily populated areas had legal training.[31] On the far northern

29. UNMSC, AGN Provincias Internas 36, p. 473, Certificación of Alphonsso Rael de Aguilar, Santa Fe, 10 January 1706.

30. Details of Gómez's life are found in UNMSC, AGN Inquisición 583, exp. 3, "Proçesso y caussa criminal contra El Sargento Mayor Fran^{co} Gómez Robledo. . . ." See also Chavez, *Origins*, pp. 35–37.

31. Mark A. Burkholder, *Politics of a Colonial Career: José Baquíjano and the Audiencia of Lima* (Albuquerque: University of New Mexico Press, 1980), aptly demonstrates this point. For Baquíjano's activities as protector, see pp. 50–54.

frontier, where schools were lacking and literacy rare, no such qualifications for office existed. To be sure, many of the New Mexico protectors often displayed hardheaded common sense, good judgment, and a rudimentary knowledge of the basic precepts of Spanish justice and legal procedure. But there is no evidence that any of them ever had any formal legal training.

As in other parts of northern New Spain, friction between civil and clerical authority highlighted affairs in seventeenth-century New Mexico. On the upper Rio Grande, however, the problems were more acute, especially in the decade of the 1660s. Following Oñate's initial failure to locate hoped-for mineral wealth, Spanish authorities considered abandoning the province. The crown, however, decided to retain the area as a mission field.[32] As a result, the clergy tended to exert more authority in New Mexico's temporal affairs than ordinarily may have been the case. While the central divisive issue in the seventeenth century involved control of Indian resources and labor, an important sidelight was the struggle for judicial supremacy between the civil and clerical arms of government.[33]

With one notable exception, that of Antonio González, the protectors in New Mexico identified closely with civil governors in challenging clerical authority.[34] The prestige

---

Steve J. Stern, *Peru's Indian Peoples and the Challenge of Spanish Conquest: Huamanga to 1640* (Madison: University of Wisconsin Press, 1982), pp. 115, 121, likewise mentions the juridical training of protectors in Peru.

32. *Recopilación*, l. 66, tít. 2, lib. 3; France V. Scholes, "Church and State in New Mexico," *New Mexico Historical Review* 11 (January 1936):27–28.

33. Scholes, *Troublous Times*, p. 24.

34. Evelyn Hu-DeHart, *Missionaries, Miners and Indians: Spanish Contact with the Yaqui Nation of Northwestern New Spain, 1533–1820* (Tucson: University of Arizona Press, 1981), pp. 45–48, describes a similar conflict over Indian labor

and loyalty of these men is evident in the action that the church took to punish them. The clergy brought their most powerful weapon, the Inquisition, to bear against two of the three known protectors. Diego Romero and Francisco Gómez Robledo faced the Holy Office, charged, among other things, with opposing the missionary efforts of the friars.[35] The Inquisition found Romero guilty of doctrinal errors and moral lapses, while Gómez successfully proved himself innocent of all charges. But perhaps a more compelling motive for these men being called before this tribunal was their staunch loyalty to civil authority and their execution of the governor's policies despite opposition from the clergy.[36]

On the other hand, Antonio González's role is not so clear. His part in the residencia of Governor López does not seem to be extraordinary, since questions pertaining to the treatment of the natives routinely comprised part of the residencia format.[37] At the same time, outgoing Governor Bernardo López de Mendizábal accused the incoming governor, Diego de Peñalosa, of using the residencia to strip him unfairly of the wealth that he had accumulated during his tenure in office. Undoubtedly, the protector's part in the residencia helped prove López's corruption as governor, and González may well have acted as much for Peñalosa as for the Indians.

on the Sonora frontier at roughly the same time, in which the protector also sided with civilian interests instead of with the Jesuit missionaries.

35. Inquisition proceedings against Romero and Gómez are discussed in Scholes, *Troublous Times*, pp. 172–78, 190–94, and are found in UNMSC AGN Inquisición 586, exp. 1 and 583, exp. 3, respectively.

36. Scholes, *Troublous Times*, pp. 195–96.

37. On the residencia, see the discussion in Chapter 4.

In all cases, then, the protector was a tool with which one faction of New Mexico's power structure sought to gain the upper hand over another. The most important confrontation, of course, was that of the civilian versus the clerical elites in their attempts to dominate the distribution and control of native labor. The residencia of López pitted one civil official against another. As González proved, the protector acting in the name of Indian rights could be a powerful weapon in the struggle for New Mexico's limited resources. As in other areas of Spanish America, defense of native rights by Spaniards sometimes, though certainly not always, coincided with personal gain or vested interest.[38]

Documentation for the activities of the protectores de indios in seventeenth-century New Mexico is sparse. Little is known of either Diego Romero or Francisco Gómez Robledo as protectors. Antonio González appears numerous times, but only in connection with one set of proceedings. While extant evidence tends to show the protectors in a generally favorable light, conditions in seventeenth-century New Mexico were decidedly unfavorable for the Indians, despite whatever good these officials may have done. Far from the eyes of high-level authority, colonists and clergy often used heavy-handed methods of controlling native labor and resources. Much has been written about the causes of the Pueblo Revolt of 1680. It is usually explained as the consequence of church–state rivalry. However, one thing is clear—Indian protection under the existing regime had broken down.

Pueblo leaders questioned the merits of a system that

---

38. See Stern, *Peru's Indian Peoples*, pp. 119–21.

seemed to offer only burdensome exploitation, with none of the ostensible cultural and political benefits. The tight control that encomenderos and missionaries exerted over Indian society greatly limited the degree to which the natives could take autonomous action to defend themselves. Under such conditions, legal institutions, including the office of protector, apparently were not viable channels for achieving equitable treatment. For whatever reasons, either by choice or because of relative inaccessibility, the Indians had not yet learned to exploit the Spanish legal system to their advantage. The great disparity between the professed ideal and the grim reality of Indian protection in seventeenth-century New Mexico looms as a major cause of the Pueblo Revolt of 1680.

3

The Eighteenth Century:
The New Order

In the years between their expulsion from New Mexico in 1680 and recolonization in the 1690s, Spaniards maintained a tenuous foothold in the region by consolidating their position at El Paso del Norte (present-day Ciudad Juárez). Sporadic and unsuccessful attempts to reconquer the upper Rio Grande Valley color this period of strained relations between natives and Hispanics. As governors Antonio de Otermín, Pedro Reneros de Posada, and Domingo Jironza Petriz de Cruzate learned, Indians in New Mexico were not yet ready to welcome the Spaniards back with open arms. Indeed, the would-be conquerors encountered stiff resistance. Meanwhile, closer to home, some Indians who had accompanied the fleeing Spaniards southward had begun to slip away from the El Paso area to rejoin their "apostate" brethren in the North.

Afraid of the harmful effects that contact with rebellious Indians might have on those living among the exiled colonists, authorities residing in El Paso sought to check not only defection of their allies, but also to discourage any enemies from coming near the settlement. Those who persisted risked harsh consequences. Such was the case of Juan Caititi (also called Paititi), a Tigua from Isleta, convicted of trying to return to his native pueblo with a female companion, Juana Nobay. For his attempted backsliding into "apostasy and idolatry," Juan Caititi received a sentence of labor for life at the mining works of Parral. This particularly harsh punishment had a dual purpose—to chastise Juan and to serve "as an example to others" who might contemplate defection.[1]

While Spanish officials meted out stiff punishments, they did so according to standard legal procedure and in the prescribed manner for rebels and apostates. Juan Caititi, for example, had the services of a defensor, Juan Sánchez Cabello, who argued on his behalf. Similarly, defensor Juan Matías Lucero de Godoy pleaded, unsuccessfully, for leniency and commutation from Governor Domingo Jironza Petriz de Cruzate (1683–86 and 1689–91) who had sentenced several Manso and Apache Indians to death.[2] There is even a vague reference to the existence of a protector during this period. Following a formal interrogation, ten Santa Ana men captured in a Spanish raid were condemned in 1687 to ten years of labor in the ore mills (*morteros*) of Nueva Vizcaya. Although no specific name is mentioned, the trial record states that their protector was present at the sentencing.[3]

During the twelve-year period of exile, Spaniards appear

---

1. SANM II:13, "Autos criminales contra Ju° caititi yndio . . . ," 22 June 1682.
2. SANM II:31, "Causa criminal q se a seguido contra los yndios Xptianos manssos . . . ," 15 March 1684.
3. SANM II:44, Sentence of ten Queres Indians, Nuestra Señora de Guadalupe del Río del Norte, 6 October 1687.

to have used the judicial system more frequently as a mechanism of control than as a means of providing royal justice for those Indians who remained loyal to Spanish rule. While there exist cases of Spaniards who were tried and punished for mistreatment of friendly Indians, the overall tenor of the period is one of little advantage for natives under the law. The colonists acted swiftly and aggressively to counter any perceived threat to their delicate position in the region, and the provincial judicial system mirrored this attitude. As a consequence, the administration of justice during the years in El Paso was undoubtedly a feature of Spanish rule that Indians feared rather than appreciated.

By the 1690s, Spaniards had stabilized and strengthened their situation at El Paso. Meanwhile, further north, the unity that had made Pueblo victory possible in 1680 had broken down. Moreover, differences between, and within, Indian villages escalated as problems continued under native rule. Times were ripe for the military reconquest and resettlement of the upper Rio Grande. Led by Diego de Vargas, the Spaniards combined the olive branch with the sword to effect the recolonization of the province. Alliances with native pueblos, guarantees of protection for those who accepted Spanish authority, and fierce military action against those who did not, marked Vargas's initial policy toward the Indians. But while the military component of this two-sided policy proved instrumental as an opening wedge for recolonization, perhaps the protective component of Vargas's diplomacy had longer-lasting consequences for Spanish–Indian relations in the province.[4]

---

4. J. Manuel Espinosa, *Crusaders of the Rio Grande: The Story of Don Diego de Vargas and the Reconquest and Refounding of New Mexico* (Chicago: Institute of Jesuit History, 1942), is the standard account of Vargas's reentry into New

With recolonization, Spanish–Indian relations in colonial New Mexico entered a new era. Although never formally articulated, a tacit agreement emerged as each group weighed its strengths and weaknesses and pondered the advantages or dangers offered by the other side. Most emphatically, the Pueblos would not tolerate the abusive conditions that had existed before the revolt of 1680. On the other hand, European goods and technology made the Spaniards valuable trading partners and military allies in countering Apache or Navajo raids.[5] For the Spaniards, now threatened by European rivals in North America, the reoccupation of New Mexico as an imperial outpost became a necessity. A balance was struck, and practical accommodation was achieved. Pueblos would accept Spanish rule, and the Spaniards would recognize basic Indian rights.

In this new era, no longer would the large *estancia* and exploitative encomienda serve as the bases of colonial land and labor systems. Instead, Vargas initiated in New Mexico the practice of land grants to smallholders who were less dependent upon native labor.[6] Since New Mexico's *raison d'être* had shifted from a mission field to that of a defensive

---

Mexico. See also J. Manuel Espinosa, trans., with notes, *The First Expedition of Vargas into New Mexico, 1692* (Albuquerque: University of New Mexico Press, 1940).

5. Jack D. Forbes, *Apache, Navaho and Spaniard* (Norman: University of Oklahoma Press, 1960), pp. 281–92, places the onus of enmity between these groups on the Spaniards who, he claims, disrupted traditional networks of trade.

6. Although the crown granted Vargas an encomienda, he never directly received tribute from the Indians. Provisions were made for his heirs to collect a yearly sum from the crown. AGI Guadalajara 70, "Papeles sentenzias y testimonios a favor de Don Diego de Bargas Zapata y luxán Ponce de león Marqués de la Nava de Brazinas." See also Lansing B. Bloom, "The Vargas Encomienda," *New Mexico Historical Review* 14 (October 1939):366–417.

bastion, the clergy would no longer dominate Pueblo life as it had in the previous century.[7] Native ceremonial life, so crucial to the fabric of Pueblo society, now came under less stringent scrutiny from Spanish authorities. Similarly, accommodation called for the end of legally sanctioned Indian tribute in New Mexico. After 1680, the Pueblos, unlike their counterparts throughout most of the Spanish colonies, paid no regular assessment.[8] Finally, the new order implicitly sanctioned certain structural components vital to Pueblo life, the most important of which were communal landholdings and the performance of rituals that did not openly conflict with European sensibilities. The cornerstone of the new order, then, was Indian acceptance of Spanish sovereignty in exchange for protection of territorial integrity and limited communal autonomy.

The return of Diego de Vargas to New Mexico also marked the renewal of the Indians' status as subjects of the crown and the beginning of a period of growing familiarity with the Spanish legal system. Throughout the eighteenth and early nineteenth centuries, the Pueblos increasingly appealed to colonial authorities to uphold their recognized rights *as Indians* under Spanish law. Furthermore, natives were remarkably aware of those laws that affected them. While this awareness is striking, it is perhaps not so surprising. Not only did the Indians begin to have more dealings with the legal system, but also, normal administrative

---

7. See, for example, SANM II:280, Petition of Félix Martínez to Padre Custodio Fray Antonio Camargo, Santa Fe, 12 January 1717.
8. AGI Guadalajara 70, "Papeles . . . de Don Diego de Bargas . . ." f. 9v.; also SANM II:420, "Residencia dada Por el señor Dn Gerbasio Cruzat y Góngora . . . ," 26 August–30 October 1737, ff. 67, 73, 92, 122v., 127, passim.

procedure called for public announcement of new laws, decrees, and edicts.[9] In some land disputes, for example, a crier announced in Spanish and native languages the various stages of procedure.[10]

The petition of Isleta Pueblo to Governor Fernando de la Concha in 1791 asking for the removal of their priest reflects this general familiarity with Hispanic law. According to the Indians, the mission father denied them the right to perform customary dances and to carry out the traditional rabbit hunt. Artfully playing the role of loyal subjects of the crown, the natives alluded to laws favoring their position. "We understand," they reminded the governor, "that Our King (may God keep him) does not deprive us of such diversions."[11] The friar retired from the province soon thereafter.

In the early years of the eighteenth century, the office of protector de indios appears as an important link between the Indian community and the Spanish legal system. As early as 1703, six Teguas protested their false imprisonment and asked that Ramón García Jurado be named protector and defensor in any future judicial proceedings.[12] No record can be found to show whether Governor Diego de Vargas

9. Marc Simmons, *Spanish Government in New Mexico* (Albuquerque: University of New Mexico Press, 1968), p. 186; SANM II:883, proclamation of Superior Orden, Santa Fe, 22 January 1784.

10. See, for instance, SANM II:595a, Sentencia of Tomás Vélez Cachupín, Santa Fe, 12 April 1765 [copy].

11. SANM II:1172, "Los Yndios y su gov.ʳ de este Pueblo de la Ysleta . . . ," [November?] 1791.

12. SANM II:93, "Petición . . . al Señor Marqués de la Naua de Brazinas," 9 December 1703. Ralph Emerson Twitchell, *The Spanish Archives of New Mexico*, vol. 2 (Cedar Rapids, Iowa: Torch Press, 1914), p. 103, lists García Jurado on the muster of Vargas's recolonization.

approved the petition, but the Indians demonstrated the importance they placed on the office for legal representation.[13]

By 1704, however, an officially named protector did exist for the natives of New Mexico. In that year, the "protector general de indios," Alonso Rael de Aguilar, acted on behalf of San Felipe Pueblo. Two Spanish *vecinos* petitioned for land in the Angostura area, located on the west side of the Rio Grande, between the settlement of Bernalillo and San Felipe Pueblo. Arguing that the pueblo's holdings exceeded the so-called pueblo league, recognized by Spanish authorities, the petitioners asked that San Felipe's land be measured and that they be granted any land found outside the square league.[14] Governor Diego de Vargas ordered the alcaldes of that jurisdiction to examine the lands in question, in the company of the protector de indios, and to report on the propriety of the vecinos' request.

The response of Rael de Aguilar illuminates not only the nature of the new order but also the future role of the protector de indios in New Mexico. The Indians had held the land since the founding of the village, claimed Rael, and used it to grow "grains for their nourishment, and,

13. Denial of the request for García Jurado would be understandable, since Ramón's father, José García Jurado, had been a leading adversary of Vargas. See Espinosa, *Crusaders of the Rio Grande*, pp. 336–39.

14. This measurement extended one league (approximately 2.6 miles) in each of the cardinal directions from a well-established fixture of the pueblo, usually the church or cemetery. However, in some cases, as in this one, considerations of terrain allowed for flexibility in measuring this distance. Although no legislation appears to establish the legal nature of the "pueblo league," repeated allusions throughout the eighteenth and nineteenth centuries indicate that Spaniard and Indian alike commonly recognized this minimum territorial guarantee.

likewise, they clothe themselves with the cotton that they cultivate. " Since the Spanish petitioners already had sufficient land on the other side of the river, Rael opined that the grant should not be made. Moreover, because of the proximity of the proposed grant to the natives' fields, the Spaniards' livestock might easily damage their crops, a clear violation of colonial law.[15] He further noted that the rugged mesa to the west of San Felipe made this portion of the village league unsuitable for agriculture. Ideally, according to the protector, the league should be comprised of whichever lands "might best benefit said natives," regardless of square measurements. As the clinching argument, Rael cited the faithfulness of San Felipe as "loyal vassals" in local Indian rebellions of 1693 and 1696 as reason enough for denying the petition.[16] Vargas had received from the *Junta General de Hacienda* in Mexico City specific instructions to reward faithful Pueblos with "privileges due loyal subjects, and . . . protection against their enemies."[17] Vargas no doubt also recognized the importance that the Pueblos themselves placed on their communal lands and repaid their allegiance to the Spanish regime by denying the vecinos' request.

Like San Felipe, the pueblo of San Ildefonso also took advantage of the presence of their protector to defend their village holdings. In 1704 they complained to their protector, Alonso Rael de Aguilar, that Captain Ignacio de Roybal had acquired by grant a tract of land they considered theirs.

15. *Recopilación de Leyes de Los Reynos de Las Indias* (Madrid: Julián de Paredes, 1681; facsimile reprint, Madrid: Ediciones Cultura Hispánica, 1973), l. 12, tít. 12, lib. 4.

16. SANM I:78, "Pleyto de Xp^al Xaramillo con los Yndios de S Ph^e," 26 February 1704.

17. Espinosa, *Crusaders of the Rio Grande*, pp. 292, 295.

The petition Rael presented to interim Governor Juan Páez Hurtado outlined their grievances and briefly described the history of the pueblo's use of the agricultural land in question. Rael closed the document with a request that the governor uphold the right of the Indians to all land within one league of each of the cardinal directions from the pueblo church. He also suggested that Roybal present his grant title for inspection.

Governor Páez, following normal procedure, ordered an investigation of the disputed area, after which he called for a new measurement to determine the extent of the pueblo's holdings. Although the local alcalde carried out the measurement, documentation relative to the proceedings ends at this point, with no mention of either official approval or disapproval of the grant. Nevertheless, San Ildefonso probably received a favorable decision. Páez noted that Roybal's grant had not been formally confirmed, and he assured the pueblo that he had taken the "necessary steps" to rectify the situation.[18]

Defense of Indian land title appears to be the most important way in which the protectores de indios exercised their office after the Pueblo Revolt of 1680, but certainly not the only way. During the administration of Governor Francisco Cuervo y Valdés (1705–7), Alonso Rael de Aguilar attended in Santa Fe the installation of newly chosen Pueblo officials. In a bid to have his appointment extended, Governor Cuervo sought, and received, from the Indians approval for his past administration. Speaking through their protector, various Pueblo leaders expressed contentment

---

18. SANM I:1339, "Petizión a favor de los Yndios teguas contra Ynacio de Roybal," 16 September 1704.

with their treatment under Cuervo's rule.[19] Perhaps the presence of the protector as a witness to the proceedings lent an air of gravity that the governor desired.

As noted earlier, those who exercised the functions of protector de indios in seventeenth-century New Mexico, while not trained jurists, were nevertheless men of importance in local affairs. After the recolonization of the province, this tendency continued. Perhaps the man who best exemplifies the second line of colonial official who often filled this position in New Mexico is Alonso (or Alfonso) Rael de Aguilar. Born in Lorca (Murcia), Spain, Rael found his way to New Spain's northern frontier sometime after the Pueblo Revolt of 1680 and soon rose to a position of prominence. Diego de Vargas appointed him secretary of government and war on 21 August 1692, in El Paso. A leading figure in the reconquest of the province shortly thereafter, Rael went on to hold a number of offices in New Mexico, including *alcalde ordinario de primer voto* of Santa Fe, protector de indios, and lieutenant general (*teniente general*) of the province.[20] The solicitude and hard work of able men like Rael de Aguilar placed Spanish rule on solid ground and provided the basis for administrative continuity from one governor to the next in colonial New Mexico. In his dealings as protector, and in his other official capacities,

19. UNMSC AGN Provincias Internas 36, p. 24; Oakah L. Jones, *Pueblo Warriors and Spanish Conquest* (Norman: University of Oklahoma Press, 1966), p. 78. Jones mistakenly claims that protectors made their first appearance in New Mexico at this time, asserting that "there is no record of their presence in New Mexico before 1706" (p. 78).

20. Rael's appointment as *secretario de gobernación y guerra* is in Espinosa's, *First Expedition of Vargas*, pp. 56–57; Angelico Chavez, *Origins of New Mexico Families* (Santa Fe: Historical Society of New Mexico, 1954), p. 263.

Rael appears to have been a conscientious and relatively disinterested administrator.

While Alonso Rael de Aguilar held the title of protector general for the province, another official apparently exercised the position, perhaps in an adjunct capacity, at El Paso. Urged by their protector in 1711, Don Santiago, "governor of the Indian pueblo of El Paso del Río del Norte," and two companions appeared before the Real Audiencia de México and complained of abusive treatment at the hands of the presidial captain, Antonio Valverde y Cossío.[21] Not only had the captain exacted unpaid labor and had beaten them, the Indians claimed, but he also had imprisoned Tiburcio Ortega, "who had been [our protector] since the time of Don Diego de Vargas until now." With Ortega gone, they were "defenseless."

Acting on the petition, the viceroy of New Spain, the Duke of Linares, ordered an investigation of conditions at El Paso. When the *juez receptor* (appointed judge) arrived in El Paso to carry out the inquest, Spaniards and a number of Indians rallied to the defense of Valverde. Vecino Juan de Alderete denied that the protector had been confined. Furthermore, rather than mistreating the Indians, Valverde had actually given them presidial supplies in times of need. Antonio Saha, an Indian, testified that a Suma leader had indeed received punishment, but this was only because of his disobedient refusal to help clean an acequia. Similar testimony from others resulted in Valverde y Cossío being cleared of all charges. Protector Tiburcio Ortega and the

---

21. Biblioteca Nacional, México (hereafter cited as BN), Nuevo México, legajo 6, núm. 11, "Autos sobre las quejas q^e han dado diferentes Yndios del Paso del Río del Norte Contra su Cap.^{n}," 10 December 1711. Valverde y Cossío later served as governor of New Mexico from 1717 to 1722.

Indians who had lodged the complaint, on the other hand, were ordered to cease their slanderous collusion, and were warned that if they continued with "such excesses," they might face four years of hard labor in a dreaded *obraje* or *mortero*.

To what extent coercion accounted for the favorable testimony is not clear, although events from Valverde's later career indicate that such may have been the case. But almost certainly, personal animosity between Ortega and Valverde played a large part in the affair. A consummate opportunist, Antonio Valverde y Cossío had parlayed little more than a driving ambition into a semiautonomous command. Sent to Spain in 1698 to further the cause of his benefactor, Diego de Vargas, Valverde at the same time had wrangled for himself the appointment of captain of the presidio at El Paso. He managed also to have himself named alcalde mayor, thereby consolidating both military and civil control of the district.[22] Later, as governor of New Mexico (1717–22), his overbearing and tyrannical rule would be the source of considerable friction in the colony. In contrast, Tiburcio Ortega's position apparently had been damaged by Valverde's self-serving machinations. In 1696 Ortega had been *regidor* and *alguacil mayor* at El Paso.[23] Both positions carried considerable weight in the community. With Valverde's subsequent rise to power, Ortega undoubtedly suffered a loss of status. Thus, his motives for acting as protector de indios in this case may well have stemmed from his injured prestige. Aside from this single incident,

---

22. Espinosa, *Crusaders of the Rio Grande*, p. 331n. 61; SANM II:76, "Cédula de su Mag^d, en que reza le onrre su Exc.^a con la Jurisdz.^on Política del passo," Madrid, 6 May 1699.
23. Espinosa, *Crusaders of the Rio Grande*, p. 271n. 51.

little else is known about the office of protector in colonial El Paso. But the tone of this affair, petty bickering over local power, more aptly reflects the legacy of the seventeenth century rather than the role which the protector would play in eighteenth-century New Mexico.

How long Alonso Rael de Aguilar held the title of protector general in Santa Fe is unclear, but by early 1712 a new official had assumed that position. Nicolás Ortiz Ladrón de Guevara's appointment to the office may have taken place as early as 1708, since this is the last date in which Rael appears as protector. The only known instance of Ortiz's activity as protector occurred in 1712, during the investigation of the allegedly seditious behavior of Juan de Tafoya, a Spaniard. According to Ortiz's representation for the Tewa pueblo of San Juan, Tafoya had passed himself off as an agent of the crown, and had duped the natives into giving him fifteen tanned animal skins (*gamuzas*). The protector asked the governor to restore the skins to the pueblo, and to release several San Juan men suspected of cooperating with Tafoya. The governor, Marqués de la Peñuela, perceiving the innocence of the Indians and the trickery of Tafoya, granted the protector's request.[24] Although nothing else is known of Ortiz's role as protector, he fits the general pattern of those who held the office in New Mexico in that he came from a prominent family.[25]

The following year, however, another individual exercised the position. Like protectores before and after, Juan de Atienza Alcalá came from distinguished parentage, and

---

24. SANM II:171, "Causa Criminal qᵉ de oficio de la Real Justizia se a seguido contra Juan de Tafoya . . . ," 26 February 1712.

25. Chavez, *Origins*, pp. 247–50.

was an active figure in local Río Arriba affairs. His father, José, was a member of the order of St. Dominic and held in New Mexico the title of alguacil mayor of the Holy Office of the Inquisition. During the first two decades of the eighteenth century, Juan de Atienza served at various times as alcalde mayor of Santa Cruz de la Cañada, and appeared as attending witness in several land transfers in the area. Unlike other protectors, Atienza was not a native New Mexican, but had been born in Puebla.[26]

The first appearance of Juan de Atienza as protector de indios involved charges of witchcraft against the ex-governor of Picurís Pueblo, Jerónimo Dirucaca.[27] According to a village resident, Dirucaca had been seen preparing a concoction of maize flour which, "after mixing, he placed in an anthill so that the ants might eat it; and just as they ate [the dough], so was eaten a corresponding portion of a girl whom he had sought, and who had resisted him until then. . . ." Brought before the Spanish governor on these serious charges, Dirucaca had assigned to him a defensor, Juan de Atienza, who promised to act "according to his best knowledge and understanding." Jerónimo Dirucaca denied in his *confesión* (declaration) the charges of witchcraft, idolatry, and cohabitation, but he must have felt that his chances for acquittal were slim. He then hit upon the perfect scheme

26. Chavez, *Origins*, p. 139; SANM II:196, "Causa Criminal . . . contra Phéliz Luján por la mala Vida que la daua a franᶜᵃ de Torres Su mujer," 14 July 1713. For activities in land transfers, see SANM I:401, Teresa de Herrera v. Diego Girón, 4 March 1706; SANM I:490, Francisco Martín v. Cristóbal Martín, 12 April 1711; SANM I:311, "Pleyto sobre unas Tierras entre Xptoual de Tafoya y Ysabel Gonzˢ," 12 June 1715.

27. SANM II:192, "Causa Criminal [contra] Gerónimo dirucaca," 8 May 1713.

to extricate himself from a rather tight jam. From his confinement in Santa Fe, he leaked word to the governor that he knew the whereabouts of a silver mine. Handcuffed, but with a promise of pardon, Dirucaca took four government officials to the canyon of Picurís, whereupon ascending a hill, they found four veins of ore, and "from all four came silver, which, it is hoped, will provide complete relief for this wretched kingdom." Finally, New Mexico would pay. Despite clearing Dirucaca of all charges, the *juez comisionado* (a magistrate appointed for a specific case), Juan Páez Hurtado, ordered him to pay court costs, and banished him to a Tewa pueblo of the suspect's choice. The decision was made known to Juan de Atienza, "his appointed attorney (*procurador nombrado*) and Protector General of the Indians of the pueblos of this kingdom."

Another instance of Atienza's activities as protector characteristically involves action on behalf of Pueblo Indians in a land dispute. Presenting a petition in the name of the Indians of Pojoaque, Atienza detailed the history of the pueblo's claim to certain lands. Apparently, Pojoaque had acquired several tracts in the immediate vicinity of the pueblo through a series of purchases from Spanish vecinos. Responding to the protector's statement, Spaniards who contested ownership then submitted to Governor Flores Mogollón memorials bolstering their respective positions. Flores, in turn, appointed Alonso Rael de Aguilar (now an alcalde of Santa Fe) to investigate and report on the matter.

At some point during the proceedings, which lasted from May 1715 to April 1716, Félix Martínez replaced Flores as governor of the province. Rael turned all the proceedings over to the new governor and, in a final statement, indicated that his commission as investigator had expired and that the protector was absent from Santa Fe. Apparently, Martínez took no further action in the case.[28] Not only was Atienza physically absent from the capital, but his thoughts lay elsewhere as well. In 1716, Atienza's father José received from the Duke of Linares, viceroy of New Spain, license for "him, his family, and sons" to leave the remote northern outpost of New Mexico. On 19 December of the same year, Juan de Atienza asked Governor Martínez to extend the life of the passport in order to forestall any possible bureaucratic red tape on the upcoming journey to Mexico City.[29] Since no further mention of Juan de Atienza is found in New Mexico documents after this date, he probably did indeed leave the province. With his departure, the protector de indios disappeared from New Mexico for nearly a century.

During the interim, however, at least two attempts to resurrect the office appear in the records. In 1747, the Count of Revilla Gigedo, viceroy of New Spain, commissioned Cristóbal Martínez to fill the position of protector de indios for New Mexico. According to the Franciscan who related the incident, Martínez actually made the long journey north to New Mexico and presented his commission to Governor Tomás Vélez Cachupín. Unfortunately for Martínez, he arrived amidst a particularly strident period

28. SANM I:7, "Pleito que puso Juan de atienza al cap^n Miguel Thenorio sobre unas tierras de pujuaque . . . ," 16 May 1715; Myra Ellen Jenkins, "Spanish Land Grants in the Tewa Area," *New Mexico Historical Review* 47 (April 1972):113–34 provides a useful overview of land ownership in the area.

29. SANM II:262, Licencia of the Duke of Linares to Joseph de Atienza Alcalá et al., México, 29 May 1715; SANM II:263, Juan Atienza Alcalá to Governor Martínez, Santa Fe, 19 December 1716. Chavez, *Origins*, notes that at least one son, José II, "el mozo," remained in New Mexico (p. 139).

in church–state relations in New Mexico.[30] The pugnacious governor informed the would-be protector that he would be confined to Santa Fe and would be powerless to impose his authority in the province. Furthermore, warned the governor, should Martínez try to exercise the duties of office, he would consider him an enemy. Unnerved, Martínez did not assume the duties of office.[31]

One apparent chronological discrepancy casts some doubt upon the veracity of this relation. The commission date of 1747 does not coincide with the years in which Vélez Cachupín served as governor. Indeed, Joaquín Codallos y Rabal served from 1743–1749, while Vélez's two terms were from 1749–1754 and from 1762–1767. On the other hand, communications in that era were notoriously slow, and it may well have taken Martínez two years to attend to necessary paperwork, make preparations, and travel the considerable distance.

Sixteen years later, in 1763, second-term governor Vélez Cachupín received a letter from the viceroy, the Marquis of Cruillas, noting that the governor still had not named a protector for the Indians of New Mexico. The letter mentions a decree of 20 May 1747, which called for the establishment of that position, and likely refers to the Martínez appointment of the previous decade. The marquis also informed Vélez that he had referred the matter to the *Auditor de Guerra* and would advise the governor of his final de-

---

30. Henry W. Kelly, *Franciscan Missions of New Mexico, 1740–1760* (Albuquerque: University of New Mexico Press, 1941), pp. 56–79.
31. UNMSC, AGN Historia 25, "Noticias lamentables acaecidas en la Nueva México," ff. 42v.–43.

cision.[32] If the Marquis of Cruillas resolved to reestablish the office in New Mexico, no subsequent action took place to carry out the decision. At the same time, officials in Mexico may have considered conditions in New Mexico to be so uncommon that strict compliance with normal procedure was not absolutely necessary in such matters.

While generalizations and comparisons between two eras for which documentation is relatively scarce can be only tentative, a few observations about the office of protector de indios help shed light on the nature of Spanish–Indian relations in the seventeenth and eighteenth centuries. Furthermore, an examination of the office reveals some characteristics of the new order established in the province after the reconquest and recolonization in 1692–93. In the known incidents involving the protector de indios in the seventeenth century, Indians did not actively solicit the aid of the protector. The natives apparently participated in the legal system in a passive rather than in an active way. In other words, aggressive pursuit of their legal rights did not characterize Indian involvement with Spanish law in the seventeenth century.

In contrast, after 1692 Indians used various methods to ensure that the terms of what might be called the "tacit agreement" of the reconquest were upheld. The most important concession that the Spaniards made was to recognize and maintain the territorial integrity of the pueblos. The natives, in turn, made active use of the legal machinery, including the protector as their representative, to pre-

---

32. SANM II:571, Marqués de Cruillas to Vélez Cachupín, México, 10 June 1763. The Auditor de Guerra was a military judge who often handled judicial affairs emanating from the northern frontier.

serve their land base. Indians took advantage of Spanish justice not just through their protector, but via a number of different officials and institutions. In the course of the eighteenth century, the Pueblo Indians of New Mexico became quite familiar with Spanish notions of justice and with methods of using the colonial legal system.

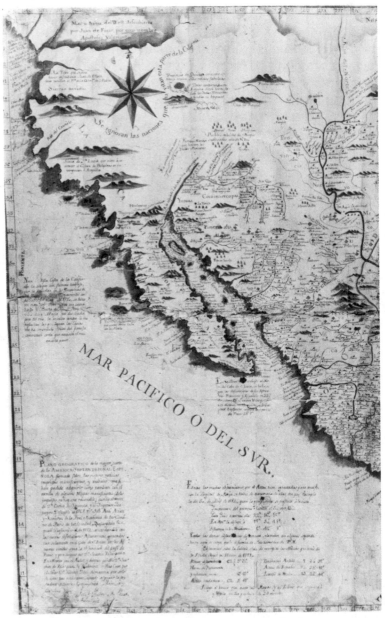

Fig. 1 "Plano geográfico de la mayor parte de la América Septentrional Española," by José Antonio de Alzate y Ramírez, 1772. Courtesy of Museo Naval (Madrid).

*H*abiendo consultado uno de los Fiscales de la Audiencia territorial de Caracas si era compatible con el actual sistema constitucional el empleo de Protector de indios, y en su caso quién debería ejercerlo; S. M., despues de haber oido al Consejo de Estado, y conformándose con su parecer, ha tenido á bien declarar que siendo por la Constitucion españoles todos los hombres libres nacidos y avecindados en territorio español, sin distincion alguna, no solo han salido los indios del estado de minoridad á que antes estaban sujetos, sino que deben ser igualados en todo lo demas á los españoles de ambos hemisferios, y por lo mismo no debe subsistir el citado empleo de Protector de indios. De Real orden lo comunico á V. para su inteligencia y efectos correspondientes.

Dios guarde á V. muchos años. Madrid 11 de Enero de 1821.

Sr. Gefe político

C. R. C.
N.º 4990

Fig. 2   Royal *cédula* and accompanying correspondence providing for the termination of the office of Protector de Indios. Archivo Histórico Nacional (Madrid), Reales Cédulas 4.990.

MINISTERIO DE LA GUERRA.

1.ª DIVISION. SECRET.ª DEL DESP.º

SECCION CENTRAL.

De orden del REY acompaño á V. *para los efectos correspondientes en* esa Capitanía General *de su cargo* un —ejemplar — rubricado —de mi mano de la circular expedida por la Secretaría del Despacho de *la Gobernación de Ultramar* á cerca de no deber ya subrogarse el empleo de Protector de Indios.

Dios guarde á V. muchos años. Madrid 19 de *Enero* — de 1821.

Cayetano Valdés.

Sr. Capitán General de Puerto Rico.

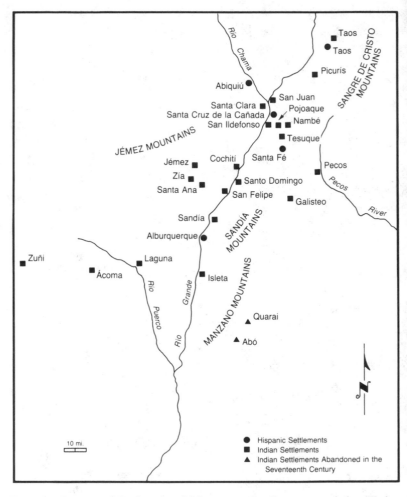

Fig. 3   Principal Indian and Hispanic Settlements of the Eighteenth Century.

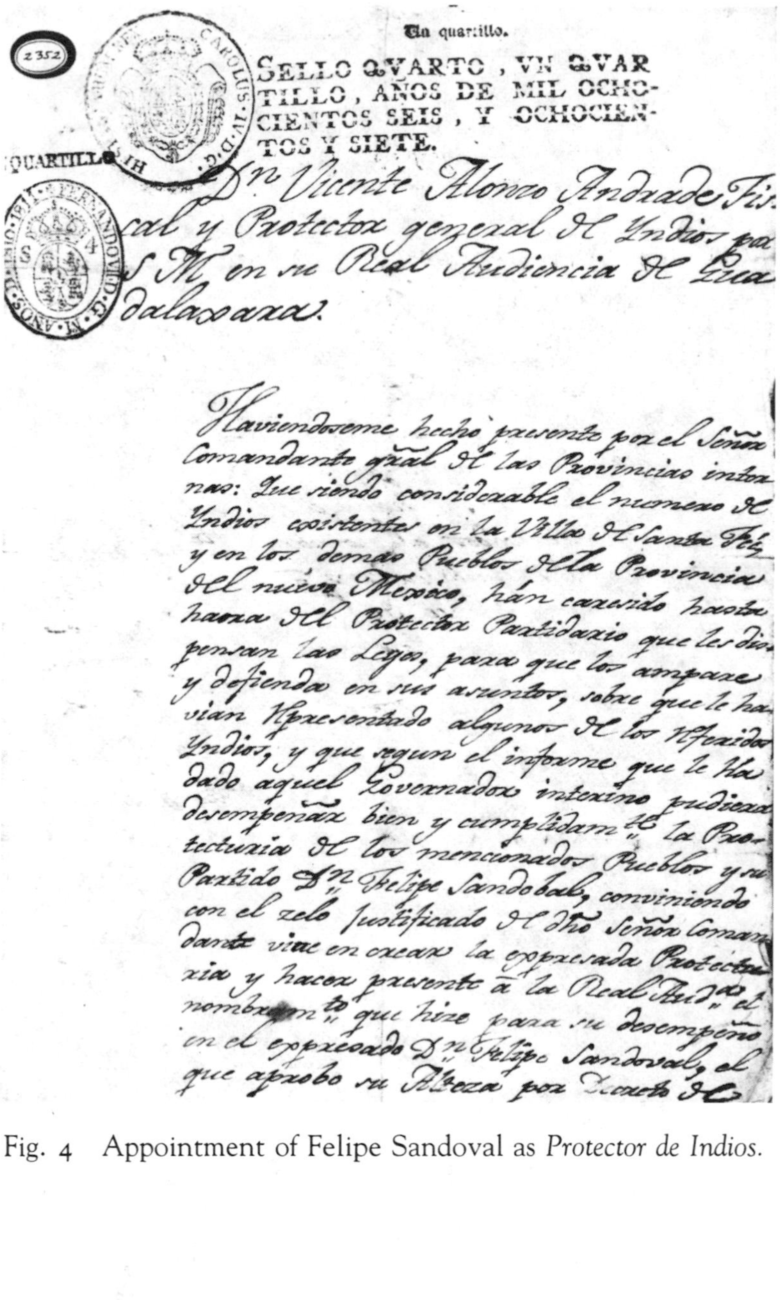
Un quartillo.

SELLO QUARTO, UN QUARTILLO, AÑOS DE MIL OCHOCIENTOS SEIS, Y OCHOCIENTOS Y SIETE.

2352

QUARTILLO

Dn Vicente Alonzo Andrade Fiscal y Protector general de Yndios por S.M. en su Real Audiencia de Guadalaxara:

Haviendoseme hecho presente por el Señor Comandante gral de las Provincias internas: Que siendo considerable el numero de Yndios existentes en la Villa de Santa Fe y en los demas Pueblos de la Provincia del nuevo Mexico, han carecido hasta haora del Protector Partidario que les dispensan las Leyes, para que los ampare y defienda en sus asuntos, sobre que le havian representado algunos de los referidos Yndios, y que segun el informe que le ha dado aquel Governador interino pudiera desempeñar bien y cumplidamente la Protectoria de los mencionados Pueblos y su Partido Dn Felipe Sandobal, conviniendo con el zelo justificado de dho Señor Comandante vine en crear la expresada Protectoria y hacer presente a la Real Audiencia el nombramiento que hize para su desempeño en el expresado Dn Felipe Sandoval, el que aprobo su Alteza por Decreto de

Fig. 4 Appointment of Felipe Sandoval as *Protector de Indios*.

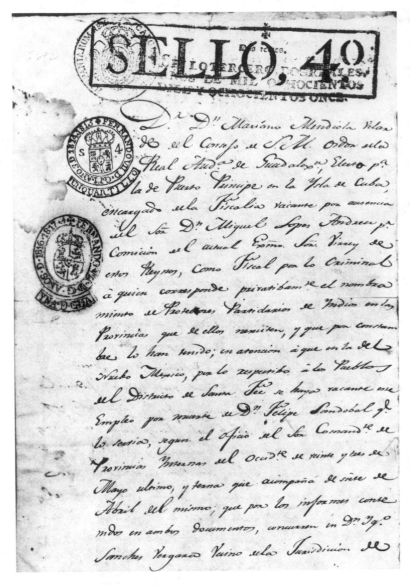

Fig. 5   Appointment of Ignacio María Sánchez Vergara as *Protector de Indios.*

Fig. 6 *From left to right:* Antonio González; Francisco Gómez Robledo; Diego Romero; Alphonsso (Alfonso) Rael de Aguilar; Nicolás Ortiz; Juan de Atienza Alcalá; Felipe Sandoval; Ignacio María Sánchez Vergara

4

Other Channels

Although the office of protector de indios seemed to disappear in New Mexico with the departure of Juan de Atienza Alcalá in late 1716 or early 1717, the concept of protection for sedentary natives lived on. Furthermore, in contrast to conditions in the seventeenth century, Pueblo Indians made active use of the Spanish legal system, particularly to deal with outsiders and to defend their recognized rights as Indians under Spanish law. Just as important was the marked shift in attitude on the part of Spanish authorities. Civil and clerical officials intruded less on native life and made a greater effort to see that the Pueblos were not exploited to the point of rebellion, as they had been in 1680.

Of course, this more lenient policy applied only to those groups who recognized Spanish authority and who lived in stable agricultural villages that fit European notions of rational government. Nomads like the Apaches, Navajos, Utes, and Comanches never really conformed to the Hispanic ideal; they remained essentially peripheral, albeit important, groups throughout the colonial period. Sedentary natives, on the other hand, had access to the Spanish legal system in a number of ways. Nearly every royal official in the New World had an implicit, and often an explicit, obligation to watch over and protect native rights.[1] When trouble arose with outsiders, and sometimes even among themselves, Indians often opted for Spanish channels of justice and sought out one of these many officials.

Pueblo groups undoubtedly resolved many village problems according to traditional native prescriptions for justice. This local autonomy, limited as it may have been, increased in the climate of accommodation that marked the new order of the eighteenth century. From time to time, however, various pueblos called on Spanish officials to settle internal squabbles. One frequent internal problem, often aggravated by Spanish presence, was that of factionalism. Spanish rule had introduced in the seventeenth century the practice of having the Pueblos elect community officials. In addition to these figures, who served primarily as spokesmen for external affairs, there existed another set of leaders who were chosen by traditional means. Those leaders sanctioned by the Spaniards tended to be more acculturated. Although the two groups of officials usually cooperated, this dual power structure perhaps increased the potential for intervillage conflict.[2] Two coexisting cultural points of view ("tra-

---

1. *Recopilación de Leyes de Los Reynos de Las Indias* (Madrid: Julián de Paredes, 1681; facsimile reprint, Madrid: Ediciones Cultura Hispánica, 1973), l. 1, tít. 1, lib. 6.
2. Edward H. Spicer, *Cycles of Conquest: The Impact of Spain, Mexico, and the United States on the Indians of the Southwest, 1533–1960* (Tucson: University of Arizona Press, 1962), p. 392.

ditional" and "progressive" in later terminology) at times led to factional strife within the native community.[3] An incident that occurred in 1771 aptly conveys this tension. It also shows the extent to which most Pueblos probably maintained traditional forms of group authority. Investigating complaints of tribal conflict at Isleta Pueblo, Alcalde Mayor Juan González Bas found that two rival power blocs existed.

Two [Indians of Isleta] . . . said that commonly among the natives of that pueblo, they have what they call a cacique, as a king, whose commands they obey; and when some matter is to be decided among the natives of the pueblo, this cacique always presides over the meetings, and they follow his opinion without the slightest opposition from the rest of the natives.[4]

Moreover, the cacique had urged his people "not to forget their ancient language which they must always conserve for the memory of their ancestors." In this case, discontent on the part of one leadership faction (the pueblo governor and his *capitán mayor de guerra*) had led to a denunciation of the powerful traditional leader, the cacique. Since Spanish rule legitimized the power of the former two pueblo officials, it is perhaps not surprising that they appealed to Spanish authority to restore their injured prestige. Punctuating the nature of the new order, however, Governor Pedro Fermín de Mendinueta did little more than to order the Isleta na-

---

3. A constant theme in Pecos Pueblo history was this animosity between the leaders of the two cultural viewpoints. John L. Kessell, *Kiva, Cross, and Crown: The Pecos Indians and New Mexico, 1540–1840* (Washington, D.C.: National Park Service, 1979), *passim*, and especially pp. 229–97.

4. SANM II:662, "Autos seguidos a pedimento del Pueblo de Sⁿ Agustín de la Ysleta contra Mariano Beitia, coyote del mismo Pueblo," 4 July 1771.

tives not to obey their cacique, and to cease using this term. Significantly, the cacique was left untouched.

Not only acculturated natives, but also tradition-minded Pueblos made use of Hispanic officials to resolve an internal power struggle. Petitioning directly to the Spanish governor in Santa Fe, Santa Clara Pueblo presented in 1788 its grievances against tribal governor Antonio Naranjo, whom they accused of mistreatment of several pueblo members. After an investigation by the alcalde mayor of the jurisdiction, Governor Fernando de la Concha removed Naranjo from office and ordered the pueblo to elect a new governor.[5]

In addition to factional quarrels, Indians often used Spanish justice within the pueblo for cases of an especially grave nature, such as murder or witchcraft.[6] Moreover, the *visita* of the Spanish governor, which will be discussed later, provided an avenue for internal grievances of a petty nature, such as settlement of debts.[7]

While Pueblos occasionally used Spanish justice internally, they routinely employed Spanish legal machinery to deal with outsiders, principally their Hispanic neighbors. Throughout the colonial period and into the present century, Indians and non-Indians contested land boundaries and water rights. Complaints to the governor and other officials about encroachment or errant livestock abound in

5. SANM II:1004, Los hijos y Naturales del Pueblo de Sta Clara to Governor, Santa Fe, 27 May 1788.
6. See, for example, SANM II:381, Proceedings against Melchor Truxillo for witchcraft, 11 February 1733; SANM II:673, "Causa criminal contra las reas Mᵃ Francᶜᵃ y Mᵃ su madre sentenciadas a muerte . . . ," 22 April 1773.
7. SANM II:470, "Autos de la Visita General . . . fechos por . . . Dⁿ Joachín Codallos y Rabal . . . ," 20 June 1745; SANM II:389, "Visita de los Pueblos de Sᵗᵃ María de Galisteo y de Nuestra Señora de los Ángeles de Pecos hecha por el Coronel Dⁿ jeruasio Cruzat y Góngora . . . ," 27 July 1733.

the colonial archives of New Mexico. Other grievances against outsiders that Indians brought to the attention of royal officials included such things as nonpayment of debts and wages, mistreatment by masters, or bodily injury.[8] While the bulk of the complaints were directed against vecinos, natives often went to Spanish authorities to demand satisfaction against Indians outside their pueblo, and, at times, against the clergy.

The official with whom the natives had most contact was the alcalde of a particular jurisdiction. Besides his military and police duties, the alcalde also had judicial powers in cases of minor consequence.[9] Indeed, the term *justicia mayor*, which applied to the same office, reflects the importance of the judicial role of the alcalde. A *teniente alcalde* carried out similar functions in a subdivision of the alcalde's territorial jurisdiction. In most minor cases, the decision of the alcalde was final. When incidents of greater severity arose, the alcalde routinely initiated the paperwork relative to a particular case—the *sumaria*. The format of the sumaria included a statement of charges, preliminary testimony by witnesses, and a declaration by the accused.[10] These documents then passed to the governor for his decision. In his

8. For examples of each, see SANM II:406a, "Pleito entre Francisco Padilla y Sebastián Gallegos, Indio Jumano," 29 October 1735; SANM II:574, "Diligencias seguidas por querella de dos Yndias Genízaras sirbientes contra sus amos," 12 October 1763; SANM II:447, "Causa Criminal de pedim⁰ del Yndio Asensio del Pueblo de Nambé conᵃ Baltasar Baca y Greg⁰ Venavides," 12 September 1743.

9. Marc Simmons, *Spanish Government in New Mexico* (Albuquerque: University of New Mexico Press, 1968), pp. 159–92, neatly summarizes the duties of alcalde. The entire work provides an excellent general framework for late colonial government in New Mexico.

10. Simmons, *Spanish Government*, p. 177.

role as local judge and court investigator, then, the alcalde was often a crucial figure in the administration of Spanish colonial justice.

Another function of the alcalde, especially important for the Indians' instruction in Spanish law, was that of proclaiming all royal edicts, laws, and decrees. Summoning the dwellers of each Spanish and Indian town to the central plaza, the alcalde or his appointed crier read in a loud and clear voice all new legislation relevant to the colonies.[11] The effects of this practice can be seen in the Indians' awareness of at least the basic tenets of Spanish law, and may partially explain the Pueblos' discernible understanding of legislation pertaining to their protection and rights.

While the alcalde was required to provide justice for all people living within his jurisdiction, Spanish or Indian, in practice he occasionally took advantage of the natives. Alcaldes were not remunerated and sometimes held the office for life.[12] As a consequence, they often used their position to improve their personal economic positions. In the eighteenth century, the clergy continued as a powerful voice against the abusive activities of alcaldes in New Mexico.[13] And frequently the Indians themselves complained directly to the governor about an overbearing alcalde.

11. For examples of decrees proclaimed throughout the province, see SANM II:883, proclamation of Superior Orden, Santa Fe, 10 March 1784; SANM II:891, proclamation of Real Orden, Santa Fe, 24 April 1784.

12. Simmons, *Spanish Government*, p. 194; but see Kessell, *Kiva, Cross, and Crown*, pp. 504–6, who provides a list of alcaldes which demonstrates that in the Pecos area, at least, the alcalde's tenure was usually brief.

13. For examples, see SANM II:394, "Causa criminal contra el capitán Bernavé Vaca Alcalde Mayor de . . . Zuñi por querella de los Yndios de los Pueblos de Ácoma, y Laguna sobre unas cambalaches y otras cosas qᶜ en ella se contiene," 21 December 1733; SANM II:367, "Causa Criminal echa contra el Alferes Ramón Garsía," 6 April 1732.

Most governors realized the importance of curbing illegal behavior by the alcaldes and usually investigated alleged instances of misconduct. An official reprimand often was the extent of punishment, but there were cases in which an alcalde was stripped of his office for having abused his powers or for having neglected his duties. In 1799, for example, alcalde mayor Manuel García de la Mora and his assistant were barred from holding any public office for the period of eight years for having failed to provide justice in their jurisdiction. The mission father at San Ildefonso had accused Juan Domingo Carache, a native of that pueblo, of having bewitched him. Instead of upholding the crown's prerogative of prosecuting this case of witchcraft, the alcaldes had let the friar conduct an informal investigation of his own that resulted in Carache's death.[14] Commandant General Pedro de Nava punished the two officials for not having taken charge of the investigation and for having "abandoned the defense" of Juan Domingo Carache. Nava also suggested that the Father Provincial remove the guilty friar, Antonio Barreras, from New Mexico. Barreras probably enjoyed ecclesiastical privilege (*fuero eclesiástico*) in this case and could not be prosecuted under civil law. But the troubled friar served only in Río Abajo after this incident.[15]

14. *Recopilación*, l. 35, tít. 1, lib. 6, defines the crown's jurisdiction in cases such as this.

15. SANM II:1462, Pedro de Nava to Governor of New Mexico, Chihuahua, 11 September 1799. *Las Siete Partidas del Sabio Rey don Alonso el nono* (Salamanca: Andrea de Portonaris, 1555; facsimile reprint, Madrid: Boletín Oficial del Estado, 1974), l. 61, tít. 6, part. 1; *Novísima Recopilación de las Leyes de España* (Madrid: 1805; facsimile reprint, Madrid: Boletín Oficial del Estado, 1976), ley 6, título 10, libro 1; l. 3, tít. 1, lib. 2. Angelico Chavez, *Archives of the Archdiocese of Santa Fe, 1678–1900* (Washington, D.C.: Academy of Franciscan History, 1957), pp. 242–43.

In a similar vein, the natives of Santo Domingo, San Felipe, and Cochití pueblos charged in 1718 that the alcalde mayor of their jurisdiction, Manuel Baca, had "bothered and mistreated" them. Taking their grievances directly to Governor Antonio Valverde y Cossío, the Indians alleged that Baca had made them work on his acequia and had whipped the governor of Cochití, "contrary to His Majesty's commands." After an official investigation, Valverde y Cossío stripped Baca of his office and condemned him to serve in two military campaigns against enemy Indians.[16] Plainly, the Pueblos understood the limits of the alcalde's authority and, on this occasion, took direct action to thwart their antagonist.

Despite abuses, however, the natives usually accepted the justice meted out by the local alcalde, and sometimes they considered this official a legitimate mediator for resolving conflict. A case that demonstrates this point occurred in 1720, when a Laguna Indian named Juanchillo killed another Indian. Investigating the incident, alcalde mayor Juan de Ulibarrí learned that the victim, Lavrián, had been caught poaching in a melon patch belonging to Juanchillo's sister. When the woman spotted Lavrián pilfering the melons and sought to apprehend him, a struggle ensued and Lavrián beat her. Juanchillo pursued Lavrián, shot him with an arrow, and dealt him a blow to the head with a rock. Ulibarrí explained to Lavrián's family the circumstances surrounding Lavrián's death, and they swore

---

16. SANM II:287, "Diligenzias fhas sobre quexas que dieron de Vejaziones que les hizo el Cap^n Manuel Baca, Alc^e m^{or} del pueblo de Cochití, los naturales de el," 13 May 1718.

before two witnesses, one Spanish and one Indian, that they forgave Juanchillo "now and in the future."[17] Ulibarrí's prestige and position as alcalde undoubtedly helped resolve the potentially retributive situation.

Despite scattered instances of Indian appeals to local alcaldes, documentation from the colonial period indicates that most Indian pleas for justice went directly to the provincial governor. Several factors may help explain this apparent preference for the governor's intervention. Many alcaldes had a vested financial interest in their territorial jurisdiction, and the economic concerns of alcaldes and natives often conflicted. Not unreasonably, when seeking justice, Indians might try to circumvent a long-standing rival and present their grievances to the governor in Santa Fe, who might be more likely to provide impartial justice. Another possible explanation for most written appeals being directed to the governor is that colonial New Mexico, like many frontier areas, was largely a nonliterate society. An alcalde settled most situations verbally, and used accepted notions of equity as a guide, rather than strict legal formulas. Finally, a personal relationship between natives and provincial governors was a distinctive feature of post-Revolt New Mexico. In a practice firmly established by Diego de Vargas in the 1690s, and reenforced by Juan Bautista de Anza three-quarters of a century later, Indians routinely brought their complaints to the Spanish governor. This

17. SANM II:311, "deligenzias hechas contra Juanchillo Yndio natural del Pueblo de la laguna sobre haver dado mu^{te} a vn Yndio de dho Pu^o llamado Lavriano," 7 September 1720.

tradition would continue through the era of Mexican rule, and into the early territorial period of New Mexico history.[18]

Among the many duties of governor was that of overseeing the administration of justice. As the highest ranking civil and criminal magistrate in the province, the governor received appeals from the various alcaldías and acted as judge of first instance in all cases of a serious nature. The governor also held exclusive jurisdiction in all judicial matters involving Indians within the alcaldía of Santa Fe.[19]

Indians often appealed successfully to the governor, as in the case of two *genízaras* who, in 1763, brought directly to Governor Tomás Vélez Cachupín grievances against their masters.[20] Upon investigating the matter, Vélez found that the Spanish masters had not properly cared for the women, nor had they instructed them in the Christian faith. Moreover, while out in the fields tending sheep, a chore fit only for males, one of the women was raped. The governor relieved the negligent masters of their servants and placed

18. See the exasperated comments of Governor William Carr Lane (1852–53), who complained that his life had become "one eternal round of appeals, written and verbal, from Mexican and Indian, and sometimes from Americans for reparations, of every description of wrongs . . . besides getting at least fifty embraces from Indians and sometimes from Mexicans." Quoted in Howard Roberts Lamar, *The Far Southwest, 1856–1912: A Territorial History* (New York: W. W. Norton and Company, 1970), p. 84.

19. *Recopilación*, l. 13, tít. 10, lib. 5; Lansing B. Bloom, transcriber, "Ynstrucción a Peralta por Vi-Rey," *New Mexico Historical Review* 4 (April 1929):180; on the office of governor in general, see Simmons, *Spanish Government*, pp. 53–87.

20. The term *genízaro* (f. *genízara*) refers to a Hispanicized Indian, usually of nomadic origin, who lived in the Hispanic fashion and formed an important segment of colonial New Mexico society. On the genízaros, see Angelico Chavez, "Genízaros," in Alfonso Ortiz, ed., *Handbook of North American Indians: The Southwest*, vol. 9, pp. 198–200.

both women in homes "where they might be instructed in Christian doctrine and customs, and be fed and clothed through household chores appropriate to their sex."[21]

Illustrating the Pueblos' circumvention of the alcalde's authority is the complaint of Taos Pueblo in 1731 against Sebastián Martín, Baltasar Romero, and others in the area who constantly let their livestock wander into the natives' fields. Sidestepping their alcalde, the "caciques, . . . governor, lieutenant [governor], and the rest of the Pueblo" presented their case before Governor Gervasio Cruzat y Góngora. Cruzat ordered the Spaniards to keep their animals at least one league from the fields of the Indians under penalty of a one hundred peso fine, and to "place as many herders as might be necessary to watch over the livestock."[22]

Another way in which the natives had access to the governor's justice was through the visita, the official inspection of the province.[23] Spanish law required the governor to go to every pueblo in his jurisdiction, Indian or Spanish, once during his tenure in office. In each community he heard the complaints of those who felt "harmed, molested, or prejudiced in any way by their alcalde mayor,

21. SANM II:574, "Diligencias seguidas por querella de dos Yndias Genízaras sirbientes contra sus amos," 12 October 1763.

22. SANM II:361, "Petisión y demanda puesta por los casiques y oficiales del Pueblo de San Gerónimo de los thaos contra el capitán Sevastián Martín, Baltasar Romero, y demás vesinos sobre los daños qᵉ resiuen por los Ganados de los referidos," 13 August 1731.

23. Guillermo Céspedes del Castillo, "La Visita como Institución Indiana," *Anuario de Estudios Americanos* 3 (1946):984–1025, provides an overview of the visita in Spanish America; on the visita's medieval antecedents, see Richard L. Kagan, *Lawsuits and Litigants in Castile: 1500–1700* (Chapel Hill: University of North Carolina Press, 1981), p. 205.

teniente alcalde, or any other person."[24] Although Indians at times used the visita to square up accounts within their own village, more often this procedure provided an opportunity to settle differences with outsiders. In general, complaints consited of unconsummated business agreements, as in the case of a Taos Indian, Esteban, who in 1745 complained that teniente Antonio Durán de Armijo owed him six pesos "for having woven, with other Indians, two blankets and a sheet." Occasionally, various Pueblo groups expressed discontent over errant livestock that had strayed onto their land and damaged their crops. In a practice reminiscent of the medieval "lawgiver" tradition, the governor often meted out on-the-spot justice without going through normal judicial procedures. Esteban, at Taos, was compensated immediately, as was Antonio, from Tesuque, who claimed that a Spanish vecina owed him "a trading knife for a large pot that he sold to her."[25]

Like the visita, the residencia afforded yet another opportunity to air complaints. By law, every governor faced this formal investigation at the end of his tenure. During the proceedings, all citizens of the jurisdiction were free to present statements relative to his conduct while in office.[26] A portion of the residencia generally dealt with the governor's activities in maintaining the legal rights of Indians.

24. SANM II:470, "Autos de la Visita General . . . fechos por . . . D^n Joachín Codallos y Rabal . . . ," 20 June 1745; *Recopilación*, l. 15, 19, tít. 2, lib. 5.

25. SANM II:470, "Visita General . . . Codallos y Rabal," 20 June 1745.

26. José María Mariluz Urquijo, *Ensayo Sobre los Juicios de Residencia Indianos* (Sevilla: Escuela de Estudios Hispano-Americanos de Sevilla, 1952), describes the various types of residencia in the colonies; *Recopilación*, tít. 5, lib. 5, covers legislation pertaining to the governor's residencia; l. 28, tít. 15, lib. 5, required that Indians be notified of the residencia.

Normally, the reply of the witnesses, prominent members of Spanish and Indian settlements, was that the governor had upheld justice for all.[27] But not always. The Indians of Pecos, for example, lodged a complaint against ex-governor Félix Martínez, among other things, for having compelled the *pecoseños* to cut, dress, and haul without payment more than two thousand wooden planks for construction of his "palace." Antonio Becerra Nieto, the judge appointed to carry out the residencia, ordered Martínez to reimburse the natives for material and labor involved in cutting and carting the lumber to Santa Fe.[28]

As for formal litigation, the governor not only had jurisdiction over the judicial affairs of Indians, but also had the power to appoint legal defense for them. Depending on the age of the defendant, the governor named either a defensor or curador as a legal representative in court proceedings. The practice of appointing a defensor was common throughout the northern frontier during the Spanish colonial period. As the name suggests, the defensor's role was primarily that of a defense attorney. While the protector de indios at times functioned in this capacity, more often the defensor was named specifically for a particular case. Typically, after the alcalde's preliminary investigation and arrest of the suspected criminal, the governor appointed a defensor to take the confesión of the defendant. Following the confesión, the defensor often, though not always, pre-

27. See AHP, r. 1654a, fr. 523–53; SANM II:420, "Residencia Dada Por el señor Dn Gerbasio Cruzat y Góngora . . . Resevidas Por Dn Juan Joseph Brizeño y Suñiga . . . ," 26 August 1737.

28. SANM II:323, "En los Auttos de demanda q^c los Naturales . . . del pueblo de los pecos . . . han seguido," 16 August 1723. Kessell, *Kiva, Cross, and Crown*, p. 321.

Chapter 4

sented arguments for leniency or acquittal on behalf of his charge, and then hoped for a favorable decision from the governor or other magistrate.[29] However, as Governor Fernando Chacón pointed out in 1802, he and his predecessors were hampered by the absence of "legal advisors, lawyers, [and] clerks who can properly conduct a [criminal] case."[30] Rigorous adherence to the finer points of formal procedure was conspicuously absent on the frontier.

The curador performed a function similar to that of the defensor. Curiously, though Indians had the legal status of minors, Spanish officials in New Mexico tended to make a distinction for age in judicial matters. While a defensor represented an adult, the curador acted on behalf of those under the legal age of majority (twenty-five years). The extent to which this situation represented a departure from normal administration of justice is unclear, but a document from the 1700s indicates that perhaps a unique form of jurisprudence had evolved in New Mexico.

Two women from Cochití, mother and daughter, openly confessed to the premeditated murder of the daughter's husband. A defensor, Julián de Armijo, was named for the older woman, María Josepha; but a curador was assigned for the daughter, María Francisca, who appeared to be a minor. Seeking a second opinion before rendering a decision, Governor Pedro Fermín de Mendinueta sent the ex-

29. See SANM II:673, "Causa Criminal contra las reas Mᵃ Francᵃ y Mᵃ su madre sentenciadas a muerte con parecer de asesor," 22 April 1773; SANM II:477, "Causa Criminal de oficio de la Rl. Justicia Contra Pedro de la Cruz Indio por hauer intentado fuga, pasandose a la gentilidad de la nación Cumanches . . .," 22 February 1747.

30. SANM II:1593, [Chacón] to Real Audiencia de Guadalajara, Santa Fe, 28 March 1802.

pediente of the case to the legal advisor (*asesor*) of the commandant general in Chihuahua. The reply of the asesor is illuminating. Among other things, he pointed out that as legal minors, *all* Indians, regardless of age, required the intervention of a curador. Acting upon the asesor's advice, the governor formally changed Armijo's title from defensor to curador, and the case resumed. Both women were found guilty and, in a rare example of capital punishment, were hanged.[31]

In matters that involved them as plaintiffs, Pueblos occasionally selected a professional representative to further their cause. In the context of colonial New Mexico jurisprudence, the term professional must be used with some degree of caution. While the services of these men were remunerative, they did not make a living solely by practicing law, nor did they have any formal legal training. Unlike larger population centers of the empire, the economically backward northern frontier supported no "letrado elite."

Particularly prominent in representing the Indian population in the eighteenth century was the *procurador*, who tended also to be the alcalde mayor, of the Villa of Santa Fe. The role of the procurador in colonial New Mexico is not entirely clear. Spanish law required legal representation even for those who could not afford it, and, as early as the fourteenth century, Spanish courts had provided a *procurador de pobres* for the truly needy.[32] Certainly, an econom-

---

31. SANM II:673, "Causa Criminal contra las reas Mª Franᶜᵃ y Mª su madre . . . ," 22 April 1773; SANM II:690, Mendinueta to Bucareli, Santa Fe, 14 October 1775.

32. *Siete Partidas*, l. 20, tít. 23, part. 3.; Kagan, *Lawsuits and Litigants*, p. 13; *Recopilación*, l. 26, 27, tít. 24, lib. 2, alludes to the existence of abogados and procuradores de pobres in the colonies.

ically underdeveloped area like New Mexico would provide a ready clientele for such an office. The procurador may have served a similar function in New Mexico, and, in the absence of a protector de indios, may have acted on behalf of the natives. On the other hand, the procurador of the villa may well have been compensated in some way for his counsel to private parties.

The activities of Felipe Tafoya, referred to on at least one occasion as a *procurador público*, reflect his importance as a vehicle by which Indians gained access to the Spanish legal system. For example, when two San Juan Pueblo men appeared before him claiming that their livestock had inadvertently gotten mixed in with the presidial horse herd, Felipe Tafoya asked Governor Tomás Vélez Cachupín to look into the matter. Vélez ordered Tafoya to determine which animals belonged to the Indians so that the horses might be returned to their rightful owners.[33]

In some rather important land disputes, Tafoya functioned in much the same way as the protector de indios. As "procurador of this Villa of Santa Fe and defender named by the Indian Pueblo of San Ildefonso," Tafoya wrote petitions, accompanied the alcalde when taking boundary measurements, and argued for the Pueblo throughout the litigation with their neighbors. Similarly, Carlos Fernández represented the two Indian Pueblos of Santa Clara and San Ildefonso in litigation in the 1780s. Although serving in a similar capacity, Tafoya and Fernández appear to have done so not as protectores de indios, but as attorneys representing

---

33. SANM II:507a, Felipe Tafoya to Tomás Vélez Cachupín, Santa Fe, 10 [December] 1749. Tafoya is referred to as "procurador público de esta villa [de Santa Fe]."

specific Pueblos in specific cases. The similarities in function between the two offices in this regard are forceful reminders that protection under the legal system did not depend solely upon the protector.[34]

In addition to civil officials, the clergy also played an important role in protecting Indians from their Hispanic neighbors in all areas of Spanish America. Colonial New Mexico was no exception. The dedication and efforts of the missionaries should never be underestimated. Many clergymen spent considerable effort trying to insulate the natives from the worst features of European culture, while simultaneously inculcating their neophytes with the rudiments of Christian doctrine. Of principal concern to most missionaries, therefore, was the well-being of the mission itself. Still, the orbits of missionaries and colonists often coincided. Although the clergy remained outside civil jurisdiction, their activity relative to Indians and civil law was important in New Mexico, where no secular clergy operated and the Franciscans administered to the entire population.

As noted in the opening chapter, the clergy exercised the duties of protector de indios during the early years of Spanish colonization. Even after secularization of the office in the late sixteenth century, however, they still had the obligation to watch over and report any mistreatment of Indians. In a royal cédula of 1580, Philip II outlined this

---

34. SANM I:1351, "Autos Seguidos por los Yndios del Pueblo de S.ⁿ Yldefonso contra los Erederos de Juana Luján y de fran.ᶜᵒ Gómez deel Castillo," 4 February 1763. SANM I:1354, Las Repúblicas de Santa Clara y San Yldefonso to Anza, Santa Fe, 6 May 1786. Myra Ellen Jenkins, "Spanish Land Grants in the Tewa Area," *New Mexico Historical Review* 47 (April 1972):124–25, calls Felipe Tafoya the Indians' "protector." Although serving an almost identical function, Tafoya and Fernández appear to have acted without the formal title of that office.

function, maintaining that "as true spiritual fathers" of the new converts the clergy must not only protect the natives, but also guard their legal privileges and prerogatives. In effect, this directive reiterated an earlier decree that required the clergy to notify royal officials, including local protectors, of any mistreatment of Indians.[35]

Clerical vigilance often took the form of active participation in civil law on behalf of the Pueblos. At times, the natives went to their mission priest and asked him to put in writing some petition or statement they wished to make. In this context, the missionary served in an informal manner as scribe and procurador.[36] On other occasions, missionaries acted on their own initiative to correct injustices. In New Mexico, the clergy consistently complained about the activities of local alcaldes. These denunciations sometimes had the air of the old church–state rivalry, but usually the missionaries called attention to real abuses of power.

For example, Fray Diego de Arias, missionary at Zía Pueblo, firmly believed that his duty as mission father was to guide his flock on the "path to heaven, and in things temporal, to defend them from the bloodthirsty wolves who molest and harass them." In 1732, he accused Ramón García Jurado of having misused the powers of alcalde mayor, claiming that the natives had performed work for which García had not paid them. As a result of Fray Diego's intervention, the governor banished the errant alcalde to Zuñi Pueblo for

35. *Recopilación*, l. 1, tít. 1, lib. 6; l. 14, tít. 6, lib. 6.
36. *Recopilación*, l. 1, tít. 12, lib. 1, prohibits the clergy from carrying the titles of alcalde, escribano, or abogado.

two years and forced him to pay the Zías for their labor.[37] As this incident demonstrates, even in the realm of civil jurisdiction the clergy could exert considerable influence to protect the Indians.

Sedentary natives living under Spanish rule in colonial New Mexico had access to the legal system in a variety of ways, even during the period in which the office of protector de indios lay dormant. The numerous means by which Indians made use of Spanish justice evidently made this system viable for resolving conflicts, principally disagreements with their Spanish neighbors. In pursuing these other channels of justice, the Pueblos displayed their characteristic willingness to accept those elements of alien culture that benefited community needs. Aware of the rudiments of Spanish law, they often appealed to their rights as Indians in order to preserve those components of communal life essential to their cultural identity, particularly their lands and customs.

In a sense, this selective borrowing had contradictory effects. On the one hand, Indians became at least partially Hispanicized because of their recognition of Spanish sovereignty and their acceptance of Hispanic jurisprudence. On the other hand, their use of Spanish legal machinery served to counteract attacks on their community lands and traditional customs. Thus, it preservd the communal quality of Pueblo culture that has persisted to this day.

Although the protector was absent during much of the eighteenth century, the period proved to be an important

---

37. SANM II:367, 370, 378a, 380, "Causa Criminal echa contra el Alférez Ramón Garsía," 22 July 1732 (two *cuadernos*). Ironically, García appears to be the same person that six Tiguas had requested for their protector in 1703.

one. Persistent use of various channels available to Indians throughout the century familiarized the natives with the methods and procedures of Spanish law. Indeed, the Pueblos' general knowledge of pertinent legislation was the product of decades of dealing with Hispanic justice. This familiarity with the judicial machinery was the principal reason for the reestablishment of the office of protector de indios in the early nineteenth century.

5

The Nineteenth Century:
Continuity and Change

Throughout the eighteenth century, the Indian population of New Mexico learned to use the mechanisms of Spanish legal justice to their advantage. Indeed, despite the rapidly growing Hispanic population, Indian communities enjoyed relative success in protecting their land base and certain communal traditions from outside disruptions. At the same time, natives residing in Spanish towns or working for Hispanic employers likewise used royal justice in both civil and criminal cases. This familiarity with the system continued into the nineteenth century.

The man who perhaps best embodies the natives' knowledge and use of Spanish law in nineteenth-century New Mexico is José Quintana (sometimes called Juan José Quintana) of the Pueblo de Cochití. Reflecting the degree to which Indians grasped the workings of the system, Quintana often opted for Spanish justice for his personal interests as well as for those of the pueblo.[1]

Largely as a result of José Quintana's efforts, the office of protector de indios resurfaced in New Mexico. Early in 1810, Quintana made the long journey to Chihuahua on behalf of his fellow villagers at Cochití to request that a protector be named to aid them in their affairs. Felipe Sandoval, a prominent New Mexican from Río Arriba, was Cochití's expressed choice for the position. Commandant General Nemesio Salcedo acted upon the pueblo's petition by requesting that interim Governor José Manrique send information regarding Sandoval's qualifications for office.[2] Manrique enthusiastically endorsed the nominee, and the commandant general forwarded the paperwork to the Audiencia of Guadalajara, which approved all such positions.[3] On 20 August 1810, the *protector general* of the audiencia cited the considerable number of Indians in the province of New Mexico and "the lack, up to now, of a protector" and named Felipe Sandoval *protector partidario* (that is, protector of the *partido*, or district) for the Indians of the Villa of Santa Fe and "the rest of the pueblos of New Mexico." Curiously, one of the pueblos specifically mentioned was the genízaro settlement of Santa Rosa de Abiquiú. Sandoval was to exercise the office "with the same prerogatives as the rest of the Provincial Protectors." In New Mexico, local

---

1. For Quintana's legal activities as an individual, see SANM II:2738, no. 48, "El Yndio de Cochití Juan José Quintana pide se le dé la parte de herencia que le toca a su muger," 22 April 1819; SANM II:2738, no. 56, "Juan José Quintana Yndio de Cochití reclama un macho que se le perdió y lo halló en la manada de D Pablo Montoya y con el fierro trasgerrado," 18 May 1819.

2. SANM II:2305, Salcedo to Manrique, Chihuahua, 21 March 1810.

3. SANM II:2325, Manrique to Salcedo, Santa Fe, 31 May 1810.

alcaldes publicized the appointment to the Indian and Spanish residents of their jurisdictions.[4]

Like his eighteenth-century counterparts, Felipe Sandoval Fernández de la Pedrera came from prominent parentage and was active in local affairs. His name appears in numerous property transactions, and he figured as a leading member of two important *cofradías* (lay brotherhoods).[5] While Governor Manrique considered him faithful and sufficiently intelligent for the position, Sandoval, like others on the frontier, lacked formal juridical training. In representing Indian litigants, however, Sandoval likely had first-hand knowledge, for his stepfather appears to have been none other than Felipe Tafoya.[6] As a protector de indios, the new appointee devoted most of his efforts to representing various Indian pueblos in land disputes.

One of the first cases in which Felipe Sandoval intervened on behalf of the Indians occurred in 1812, when the governor and lieutenant governor of Jémez Pueblo presented themselves before the new protector to protest what they deemed to be an unauthorized land sale by a pueblo member to the local Spanish alcalde. Since the land in question fell within the pueblo's communal square league, according to the natives, the transaction should be declared null and void. Considering their argument and request justified, Sandoval asked Governor José Manrique to take appropriate

4. SANM II:2352, Appointment of Felipe Sandoval, protector de indios, Guadalajara, 20 August 1810.

5. Archives of the Archdiocese of Santa Fe (hereafter cited as AASF) accounts 79 and 80; John L. Kessell, *Kiva, Cross, and Crown: The Pecos Indians and New Mexico, 1540–1840* (Washington, D.C.: National Park Service, 1979), pp. 434–36.

6. Angelico Chavez, *Origins of New Mexico Families* (Santa Fe: Historical Society of New Mexico, 1954), p. 283.

action to remedy the situation. Manrique forwarded the proceedings to the asesor in Chihuahua for an opinion, a practice that had been standard procedure since the 1776 administrative reorganization of the northern frontier.[7] No further documentation has surfaced to verify the outcome of this dispute, but it is clear that the natives wasted little time in turning to the newly reinstated protector.[8]

Pueblos called upon Felipe Sandoval to represent them not only against Spaniards, but also against other Indian groups. A complicated dispute between Santa Ana and San Felipe pueblos in 1813 illuminates the awkward position in which Sandoval found himself as protector of all Indian pueblos in New Mexico. According to Santa Ana, members of San Felipe had sold land to Spaniards that the former pueblo had acquired through purchase. This tract lay along the Rio Grande just south of the Angostura, approximately halfway between the two villages. Besides selling the land, Santa Ana alleged, natives of San Felipe had been cutting firewood on the disputed property. Felipe Sandoval therefore submitted the petition of Santa Ana pueblo, asking Governor José Manrique to resolve the matter.

In response, Manrique sent an official party headed by José Pino, alcalde of the jurisdiction of Albuquerque, to investigate and settle the issue. Pino seemingly arranged a solution that satisfied all. A week later, however, tribal

7. On the creation of the *Provincias Internas,* see Luis Navarro García, *Don José de Gálvez y la Comandancia General de las Provincias Internas del Norte de la Nueva España* (Sevilla: Escuela de Estudios Hispano-Americanos de Sevilla, 1964); Marc Simmons, *Spanish Government in New Mexico* (Albuquerque: University of New Mexico Press, 1968), p. 86.

8. SANM I:1355, Petition of Felipe Sandoval for the governor of Jémez Pueblo, Santa Fe, 28 August 1812.

leaders of San Felipe asked the protector to present to Manrique a statement renouncing Pino's decision. The heirs of Cristóbal Baca had sold them the land, San Felipe argued, and any lots that the pueblo may have disposed of had been done so legally. No one had opposed the sale at the time. Furthermore, they contended, in his earlier settlement Alcalde Pino had erroneously established the new boundary some five hundred varas above where it should have been.[9] Finally, they requested that Sandoval go to the disputed area and personally investigate their claims before sending the petition to Manrique. The protector did so and found San Felipe's arguments to be sound.

In the ensuing weeks, the governor ordered another investigation, this time under José María de Arze, which brought a satisfactory, if brief, end to the problem. Throughout the proceedings, the protector de indios routinely made statements for the natives (but only for San Felipe), accompanied Spanish and Indian officials who took measurements, and witnessed the signing of a compromise agreement between the two pueblos on 7 June 1813.[10] An official investigation of this type, although not formal litigation, reveals the curious position of the protector as advocate of two contending pueblos. Obviously, one village might well benefit at the expense of the other.

Felipe Sandoval also figured in only a minor role as protector de indios in a land dispute between Taos Pueblo and its surrounding vecinos. The case involved encroachment by both sides, and Sandoval's part in the affair was limited to making one statement for the Indians. Early in the pro-

9. A vara is a linear measurement approximately 32.9 inches long.
10. SANM I:1356, Santa Ana v. San Felipe, 5 May 1813.

ceedings, Sandoval suggested that, in fairness to both sides, a "renter's agreement" (*composición de arrendatario*) be reached between the interested parties. At the same time, however, the protector pointed out that the tract in question was within the Taos league, and that "the vecinos who may have purchased within that tract do not have a right to the land that belongs to the cited pueblo."[11] One wonders why Sandoval played such an inconspicuous role in this particular case. Yet one must bear in mind that Indians used the services of the protector at their own discretion. Although several explanations are possible, Taos Pueblo may have decided that a "renter's agreement" was unacceptable, and that Sandoval was not the best person to present their arguments.

In 1815, several prominent Santa Fe residents, led by Juan de Dios Peña, petitioned for vacant land in the vicinity of Pecos Pueblo. Settlement at this site, the would-be grantees contended, would "serve as a buffer against the enemy Apaches and other wild Indians." Upon reviewing this request for land just north of the village, "along both sides of the river," Governor Alberto Máynez directed the *ayuntamiento* of Santa Fe to determine the possibility of encroachment should the grant be made. In response, protector Felipe Sandoval investigated the proposed grant and indicated that the land in question was well outside the pueblo league, and that it therefore could be settled without harm

---

11. SANM I:1357, Sandoval to governor, Santa Fe, 15 April 1815. For a broader view of land tenure in the Taos Valley, see Myra Ellen Jenkins, "Taos Pueblo and Its Neighbors, 1540–1847," *New Mexico Historical Review* 41 (April 1966):85–114.

or prejudice to the natives of Pecos.[12] No further action was taken at that point, but the following spring, Juan de Dios Peña again asked for land, this time to the west, "well outside the holdings of the pueblo."[13] Governor Máynez ordered the protector to report. The proposed site, said Sandoval, was "independent of the league and farmland of the natives."[14] With this affirmation, the governor acceded to the petitioners' request, but stipulated that they be given only the land that they might cultivate and fence.[15]

Under what circumstances did Sandoval make this less-than-vigorous defense of Pecos land? Possibly, as one scholar has suggested, "close political connections between Protector Sandoval and the [grant] applicants" account for don Felipe's actions.[16] More probably, Sandoval may have felt that the grant was justifiable. By the second decade of the nineteenth century, Pecos was a dying pueblo. The once

---

12. SANM I:703, Petition of Juan de Dios Peña, Santa Fe, 9 August 1814; Felipe Sandoval to governor, Santa Fe, 17 August 1814. See also Kessell, *Kiva, Cross, and Crown*, pp. 441–42.

13. New Mexico State Archives and Records Center, Records of the U.S. Surveyor General (hereafter cited as SG):18, Juan de Dios Peña to [Máynez], Santa Fe, 28 March 1815.

14. SG:18, Statement of Felipe Sandoval, Santa Fe, 28 March 1815. G. Emlen Hall, *Four Leagues of Pecos: A Legal History of the Pecos Grant, 1800–1933* (Albuquerque: University of New Mexico Press, 1984), p. 22, makes a legal point of this document, claiming that Sandoval "added a farmland qualification to the pueblo's league that no formal Spanish law required." This insight appears to be based upon a misreading of the phrase "legua y lavor," which he has rendered "league of farmland." If anything, the phrase seems to imply the recognition of any productive farmland *outside* the natives' league.

15. SG:18, Decreto of Máynez, Santa Fe, 29 March 1815.

16. Hall, *Four Leagues of Pecos*, pp. 22–23, points out that Sandoval, Peña, and Juan Ortiz (a coapplicant for the grant) were fellow ayuntamiento members.

mighty village, which had boasted a population of roughly 800 in 1695, had dwindled, by one count, to "no more than 40 persons" in 1815.[17] If otherwise unproductive agricultural land could be put to good use, and a defensive outpost be established at the same time, then so much the better. Significantly, Sandoval never took similar action when dealing with other, more vibrant Indian communities. If the protector's intentions regarding Pecos might be questioned, not so with Cochití. Perhaps the most interesting, and by far the most completely documented case in which Sandoval served as protector was that of the Pueblo de Cochití against Luis María Cabeza de Baca. A close study of this case sheds considerable light on the workings of the colonial legal system in the early nineteenth century.[18] The suit brought by the natives of Cochití involved two tracts of land, both occupied by Spanish vecinos—the Rancho de Peñablanca and the Ojo de Santa Cruz.

A complex series of grants, sales, and other land transfers dating from 1703 to 1806 had been carried out between Indians and Spaniards in these two areas. The result was the creation of a legal labyrinth. By 1815, the natives of Cochití had formally disavowed a sale that some of their village members had made to Cabeza de Baca, claiming that the transaction was the result of intimidation and fraud. At the same time, Santo Domingo Pueblo, just south of

17. Populations for Pecos, with corresponding sources, are given in Kessell, *Kiva, Cross, and Crown*, pp. 489–92.

18. The expediente relative to this case is found in the Archivo de la Real Audiencia de Guadalajara, Biblioteca del Estado de Jalisco, México (hereafter cited as ARAG), Ramo Judicial-civil 261-15-3564, "El Común del Pueblo de Cochití diciendo de nulidad a la venta de un Rancho cituado en su fundo legal, y reclamando la usurpación de otro . . . ," 26 September 1816.

Cochití, asserted that their legitimate boundaries had been inaccurately measured during the course of an earlier land transfer. Thus, they felt themselves entitled to some of the property in dispute.

Felipe Sandoval presented statements outlining the positions of both pueblos. Speaking through their protector, Cochití declared that Baca had removed boundary markers and had threatened personal harm to any Indians who tried to oppose his activities. In April 1815, Governor Alberto Máynez decreed that "Baca must immediately depart from said boundaries, leaving [his] houses and farmland to the pueblo, since they are improperly established and without authorization."[19]

But Baca did not leave, and Juan José Quintana, along with several other Cochití Indians, again made the long trek southward. This time they journeyed to Durango, to seek justice at a higher level. There they had access to the protector de indios of Durango, José Joaquín Reyes. Obviously a man with formal legal training, Reyes argued well for the natives of "Cuchipi." He enumerated the many laws favorable to Indians that had been broken or ignored in the case. Not only had their pueblo league been violated, but Baca's livestock had repeatedly damaged the natives' fields. Regarding the league, Reyes noted that Indians had only the "enjoyment of it, but not the freedom to sell, give away, or alienate it."[20] Furthermore, the consent of the Indians, their protector, and a qualified judge had to precede any sale. Reyes reiterated their status as minors. "Because

---

19. ARAG Judicial-civil 261–15–3564, "El Común del Pueblo de Cochití . . .," f. 69.

20. ARAG Judicial-civil 261–15–3564, "El Común del Pueblo de Cochití . . . ," ff. 72–73.

of their condition," he noted, they "enjoy the privilege of minors, in consideration of which . . . they cannot deal in any way without the intervention of a guardian, overseer, or their protector."[21] Finally, Reyes cited Baca's unauthorized use of force against the natives. He had imprisoned them, put them in stocks, and whipped them for no other reason, according to the protector, than having "reproached [Baca] for the improper use he makes of their water for his fields."[22]

Reyes's arguments reflect the continued perception of Indians as legal minors during the early nineteenth century. Despite incipient liberalist notions that called for equality, which found their way into the Spanish Constitution of 1812, natives continued to enjoy special protective legislation. Decrees such as that of 15 October 1810, asserting the equal status of all residents of Spanish dominions, were revoked shortly after their promulgation. They had relatively little immediate impact upon colonial law.[23]

Just as revealing are the arguments of Cabeza de Baca's defense attorney in Durango, Rafael Bracho. Expressing the probable attitude of many actual settlers, Bracho decried the principle of "privilege of the Indians," insisting that, under its guise, the natives usually caused some sort of harm.[24] He also pointed out, significantly, that the Indians had access to a number of local channels to resolve problems

21. ARAG Judicial-civil 261–15–3564, "El Común del Pueblo de Cochití . . . ," f. 78.
22. ARAG Judicial-civil 261–15–3564, "El Común del Pueblo de Cochití . . . ," f. 79.
23. The decree is found in SANM II, Orders and Decrees, r. 22, fr. 490, Real Decreto, 15 October 1810.
24. ARAG Judicial-civil 261–15–3564, "El Común del Pueblo de Cochití . . . ," f. 93.

of personal injury and damage to property. There was no need, according to Baca's attorney, to pursue these matters at a higher level. Finally, Bracho provided a telling commentary on the nature of legal procedure in the sparsely populated borderlands. Reminding the commandant general that the land sale and formation of the expediente were carried out in New Mexico, the attorney noted that on the frontier "very few contracts and judicial acts would remain standing . . . if we were to examine them for conformity to the law. 'Known truth and good faith' is the cardinal rule of those inhabitants."[25]

The asesor in Durango deferred judgment in the case, rightly pointing out that appeals should go directly to the corresponding audiencia. Somehow, the expediente of the proceedings wound up at the Juzgado General de Indios in Mexico City, though it should have gone directly to the Audiencia of Guadalajara.[26]

In what must have been the adventure of a lifetime, five sons of Cochití also arrived in New Spain's viceregal capital to seek higher justice. Representing himself as a "retired captain of the king's troops in the continual wars against the Apache nations," Antonio Quintana of Cochití (perhaps related to José?) dutifully appeared at the Juzgado General de Indios, "without an interpreter because of his knowledge of Castilian," and requested that their case be

25. ARAG Judicial-civil 261–15–3564, "El Común del Pueblo de Cochití . . . ," ff. 94–95.

26. The Audiencia of Guadalajara, the jurisdiction of which included New Mexico, had no juzgado de indios as did the Audiencia of Mexico, but reviewed directly appeals involving Indians. See Woodrow Borah, *Justice by Insurance: The General Indian Court of Colonial Mexico and the Legal Aides of the Half-Real* (Berkeley: University of California Press, 1983), p. 329.

carried on by an authorized legal representative. He also asked for funds for the return trip of the pueblo contingent. Both requests were obliged.[27] Ultimately, the officials of the juzgado duly sent the case to the Audiencia of Guadalajara, where Cochití received a favorable judgment. The tribunal ordered Luis María Cabeza de Baca to pay court costs and to vacate the disputed tract.[28]

Still, Cabeza de Baca never left Peñablanca, as evidenced by various letters he sent from the site during the period of Mexican sovereignty.[29] Why he failed to vacate is unclear, since provincial officials plainly knew about the assessment of court costs. Perhaps the turmoil of independence and the establishment of a new government allowed Cabeza de Baca to take advantage of the situation and ignore the audiencia's decision. For whatever reasons, Baca stayed in the area.

This important case reveals much about the relationship of Pueblo Indians to the Spanish legal system. First, the machinery of colonial justice was readily accessible. Failing to find satisfaction at the local level, Cochití carried this case to the highest possible judicial authority. A rep-

27. ARAG Judicial-civil 261–15–3564, "El Común del Pueblo de Cochití . . . ," ff. 2–4.
28. SANM I:1283, Auto of the Real Audiencia de Guadalajara, Guadalajara, 16 [?] 1819; SANM I:1284, Melgares to García Conde, Santa Fe, 19 June 1820, and Melgares to Real Audiencia de Guadalajara, Santa Fe, 19 June 1820.
29. See, for example, New Mexico State Archives and Records Center, Mexican Archives of New Mexico (hereafter cited as MANM), r. 3, fr. 769–70, Luis María Cabeza de Baca to Gobernador Político, 20 February 1824. Ralph Emerson Twitchell, *The Spanish Archives of New Mexico*, vol. 1 (Cedar Rapids, Iowa: Torch Press, 1914), p. 376, asserts that Baca died at Peñablanca in 1833.

resentative specifically appointed for the purpose of litigation—the protector de indios—played a major role in each
of the successive levels of jurisdiction to which the case
devolved. Just as significant, the success of Cochití was a
direct consequence of its involvement with the Spanish
legal system. The familiarity with, and use of, available
legal channels bolsters the notion that the natives eagerly
took part in the system. They were not merely passive
participants. Instead, Indians initiated litigation to uphold
their rights under Spanish law. Finally, the willingness of
the Cochití people to undertake the arduous and expensive
journey to the viceregal capital demonstrates their confi-
dence in the system. Such an endeavor would not likely
occur to people who saw no chance of success. Certainly,
the pueblo perceived the dispute to be important, but by
no means was it a matter of immediate survival for its
members. Cochití's decision to pursue Spanish justice appears to be firmly grounded upon the belief that its land
claim was valid under existing Spanish colonial law.

Indians in New Mexico were again without a full-time
legal representative when Felipe Sandoval died suddenly in
early December 1816, leaving a vacancy in the office of
protector partidario de indios.[30] After notification and rec-
ommendation of a new candidate by the commandant general of the district, the *fiscal de lo criminal* and protector of
Indians of the Audiencia de Guadalajara, Mariano Mendiola Velarde, on 21 June 1817 named Ignacio María Sán-

---

30. AASF, Santa Fe Burials-52, f. 18 gives the date of Sandoval's interment
as 9 December 1816.

Chapter 5

chez Vergara to fill the position.[31] As protector partidario, Sánchez's instructions called for him to intercede on behalf of the natives, both collectively and individually, in whatever defense they might need of their persons or goods, and to protect them "judicially and extrajudicially" according to the laws of the Indies. The fiscal de lo criminal reiterated the protector's responsibility to report on the condition of the Indians, the treatment they received, their religious instruction, the existence of any Indian slaves in Spanish households, and instances in which land might wrongfully have been taken from any Indian pueblo.[32]

Ignacio Sánchez Vergara followed the general pattern of those who had held the office in New Mexico before him. He was a well-known figure who had long been politically active in the province. As a young man, he lived at Zuñi Pueblo with his brother Fray Mariano José Sánchez Vergara, the controversial *custodio* of the province. Later, he moved to Ácoma and Isleta, and by 1808 he held the office of alcalde mayor of the jurisdiction of Jémez.[33] In the Mexican period, Sánchez served as alcalde of the Sandía district. Unlike most of his predecessors, however, Ignacio Sánchez Vergara appears to have been as contentious as his friar

31. The duties of protector had been assumed by the fiscal de lo criminal in some jurisdictions, including the Audiencia of Guadalajara, by a royal cédula of 6 April 1776. See Concepción García-Gallo, *Las Notas a la Recopilación de Leyes de Indias, de Salas, Martínez de Rozas y Boix* (Madrid: Ediciones Cultura Hispánica del Centro Iberoamericano de Cooperación, 1979), p. 103; see, also, José María Mariluz Urquijo, *Ensayo Sobre los Juicios de Residencia Indianos* (Sevilla: Escuela de Estudios Hispano-Americanos de Sevilla, 1952), p. 158n. 13. The fiscal de lo criminal apparently confirmed appointments of protectors at a lower jurisdictional level.

32. SANM II:2692, Appointment of Sánchez Vergara, protector de indios, Guadalajara, 2 July 1817.

33. Chavez, *Origins*, p. 282.

brother, for he was constantly at odds with a number of Pueblo groups of the Río Abajo area. Allegations relative to his conduct ranged from extortion to tampering with land titles, but the tenor was usually the same—Sánchez Vergara made a career out of taking advantage of his position as alcalde.[34]

Although the new protector frequently differed with neighboring Indians, he managed to exercise the office in a somewhat circumspect manner and seems to have performed adequately in this capacity. Sánchez, for example, verified the claim of several Laguna Indians in a dispute with their Spanish neighbors over the so-called Paguate tract.[35] Moreover, he is the only protector known to have sent a report on the spiritual condition of the Indians of the province to the audiencia, one of the duties of office.[36] Sánchez's assessment of the "deplorable state and backwardness" of the natives in doctrinal matters may have been an indirect appeal for more funds on behalf of his brother, who was, of course, a Franciscan missionary.

Most of Sánchez Vergara's activities as protector, however, revolved around the continued controversy between the pueblos of Santa Ana and San Felipe over land in the Angostura area. Although the quarrel apparently had been resolved during Felipe Sandoval's tenure as protector, the

34. See SANM II:2140, Sánchez Vergara to Máynez, Santa Ana, 3 August 1808, for extortion; SANM I:1375, Statement of Rafael Miera, Bernalillo, 15 May 1829, for tampering.
35. SANM I:1373, Statement of Sánchez Vergara, Jémez, 1 June 1820. For in-depth treatment of the dispute, see Myra Ellen Jenkins, "The Baltasar Baca 'Grant': History of an Encroachment," *El Palacio* 68 (Spring and Summer 1961):47–64, 87–105.
36. SANM II:2715, Auto of the Real Audiencia de Guadalajara, Guadalajara, 27 March 1817.

issue came to the attention of the Audiencia of Guadalajara, which in 1818 had decided that the San Felipe people had indeed sold to Spanish vecinos land that was not rightfully theirs. [37] The real estate in question was to be restored to Santa Ana, and those Spaniards who had been dispossessed were to receive other lands from the royal domain. [38] The protector, Ignacio Sánchez Vergara, carried out the instructions of the audiencia in April 1819. Acting with the alcalde mayor of Alburquerque, José Mariano de la Peña, the two attempted to settle the long-standing boundary dispute between the two pueblos. The alcalde offered compensatory land in the vicinity of Socorro to the Spanish farmers caught in the middle of the conflict. [39] Peña's report to Governor Facundo Melgares indicated that the natives of Santa Ana and their protector were satisfied with the arrangement but that San Felipe was not. Sánchez Vergara also filed a separate report of the proceedings. [40]

Unhappy with the turn of events, and exercising their prerogative in the use of the protector, San Felipe now complained about the information that Sánchez had supplied to the audiencia, which had upheld Santa Ana's claim, and asked Governor Melgares to remedy this perceived injustice. [41] Despite the pueblo's dissatisfaction, the governor

37. SANM II:2715, Auto of the Real Audiencia de Guadalajara, Guadalajara, 27 March 1817.
38. SANM I:1363, Auto of the Real Audiencia de Guadalajara, Guadalajara, 14 January 1819.
39. SANM I:1364, Sánchez Vergara to Governor, Jémez, 14 April 1819.
40. SANM I:1365, Peña to Melgares, Rancho Anaya, 8 May 1819; Sánchez Vergara to Melgares, Santa Ana, 9 May 1819.
41. SANM II:2738, no. 54, "El Gobernadorcillo de San Felipe Juan de Jesús Martín en unión de los principales de dicho pueblo se presentan contra su Protector . . . ," 10 May 1819.

ordered San Felipe to make restitution to those who had bought land from them and sent Peña and Sánchez back to persuade the pueblo to abide by his decision. Relenting on its previous stance, San Felipe gave the farmers land that it had acquired by purchase in the Algodones area, just south of the pueblo on the east side of the river. No agreement could be reached, however, with one of the vecinos, Juan Bautista González. González had desired a site known as the Cubero tract, between San Felipe and Santo Domingo, as compensation for the land in Angostura, but both pueblos produced written title to a grant that Governor Pedro Fermín de Mendinueta had made to them in 1770. Peña decided that the Indians had a legitimate claim to Cubero and that it should not be given to González.[42] There is no evidence that an accord was ever achieved between San Felipe and the hard-to-please vecino.

While almost all of Sánchez Vergara's activity as protector involved land disagreements of some sort, in one case he represented an Indian in a dispute over sheep given in partido.[43] Bringing suit through a legal representative in the fall of 1819, Manuela Carrillo charged that Agustín Beitia, a native of Isleta Pueblo, had failed to repay the number of sheep he had promised in a signed agreement. Arguing persuasively for Beitia, Sánchez Vergara reminded the juez comisionado of royal legislation barring Indians, as legal

---

42. SANM II:2738, no. 68, "Don Juan Bautista Gonzales se queja de haverle despojado de su rancho en la Angostura por los Yndios de San Felipe . . . ," 6 July 1819; SANM II:2843, Peña to Melgares, Angostura, 3 August 1819.

43. SANM II:2851, Manuela Carrillo v. Agustín Beitia, 8 October 1819. The partido system was an arrangement whereby one party (A) gave to another party (B) an agreed upon number of livestock. At the end of a specified period of time, party B returned to party A the original number plus a percentage, or fixed amount, of the increase.

minors, from entering into business transactions of this type. Furthermore, he noted, Carrillo had taken advantage of the Isleta man's naïveté and hardworking nature, not only on this occasion but continually over a period of nearly twenty-five years. If Beitia were to receive the two *reales* per day for personal service as established in the *Recopilación*, Sánchez continued, the total would far exceed the meager sum of six pesos that he had actually been paid. Although the outcome of the case is unknown, Ignacio Sánchez Vergara's action in defense of Beitia appears convincing.

As Pueblos continued to use the Spanish legal system in early nineteenth-century New Mexico, events on the Iberian peninsula augured the end of the protective relationship between government and Indians. The growing wave of Enlightenment thought that had gathered momentum in Europe during the eighteenth century broke loose in the fury of the French Revolution. By the first decade of the nineteenth century, it had spilled over into Spain. In the New World, criollo society soon felt the effects of the political and social upheaval wrought by the Napoleonic invasion of the peninsula. Enlightenment ideas of equality and uniformity found their way into the legislation promulgated by the Cortes of Cádiz, culminating in the reform-minded Constitution of 1812.[44]

Egalitarian decrees were designed primarily to do away with one group's privilege over another, but the concept of privilege cut both ways. While some elites ostensibly lost

---

44. Borah, *Justice by Insurance*, pp. 396–97. SANM II, Orders and Decrees, r. 22, fr. 490, Real Decreto, 15 October 1810; and SANM I:1334, Real Decreto, 9 February 1811, are examples of such decrees of equality.

the upper hand, Indians lost the prerogatives of special protection as well. Their distinct status as minors no longer fit into current political philosophy. A brief reversion to older values marked Fernando VII's return to Spain in 1814, after a less-than-distinguished self-exile during the Napoleonic invasion. Although he annulled the acts of the Cortes, he could not stem the philosophical tide of the times, and finally, under duress, accepted the constitution in 1820.

In the wake of this reestablishment of liberal ideals, institutions and offices designed only for one group could no longer be justified. Thus, the long tradition of protection and wardship for Indians in the Spanish colonies came to an end.[45] The royal cédula abolishing the office of protector de indios appeared on 11 January 1821, in response to an inquiry from the territorial audiencia of Caracas. The question was raised: Was the office of protector de indios compatible with the current constitutional system?

His Majesty, after having heard the Council of State and agreeing with its opinion, has deigned to declare that because by the Constitution all free men born and residing in Spanish territory are Spaniards, without distinction, not only have the Indians emerged from their state of minority to which before they were subject, but also they should be equal in all else to Spaniards of both hemispheres; and for this same reason the office of protector de indios should not exist.[46]

Because of the speed of communications, news of the abolishment of the office may not have reached New Mexico

---

45. Borah, *Justice by Insurance*, pp. 385–413, offers a concise overview of the forces leading to the loss of minority status for Indians.
46. AHN, Reales Cédulas 4.990.

before the end of Spanish rule late in 1821. But a curious reference by Governor Facundo Melgares as to the status of Indians suggests that perhaps it did. The *Junta Provincial* (Provincial Assembly) sent to Melgares a dispatch dated 20 February 1821, which asked him to clarify the statement made by protector Ignacio Sánchez Vergara that the "Indians have emerged from their minority and that they now have no need of a protector."[47] However, because the cédula abolishing the office was circular (passed on from one district to another), it is unlikely that the decree had reached the northern frontier by this date. New Mexico officials may well have had in mind the general decrees of equality as set forth under the reestablished constitutional system.

What effect did the disappearance of special protection have upon the natives of New Mexico? Opinions vary on the real changes in the remote northern reaches of the new nation of Mexico. Certainly, in other parts, loss of official protection led to what one historian has called "the substitution of the tyranny of caciques and generals for the far more orderly administration of the colonial authorities."[48] Liberal thought called into question the validity of communal landholdings and, although aimed primarily at the Church, it led to dismemberment and dispossession of native village holdings.[49] Finally, the loss of special legal status denied Indians ready access, in the form of such institutions as the protector and the juzgado general de indios, to the legal system.

---

47. SANM II:2974, [Melgares] to Exma. Junta de Prov^a, Santa Fe, 18 April 1821.
48. Borah, *Justice by Insurance*, p. 412.
49. William B. Taylor, *Drinking, Homicide and Rebellion in Colonial Mexican Villages* (Stanford, Calif.: Stanford University Press, 1979), p. 147; Borah, *Justice by Insurance*, p. 412.

Disagreement persists, however, regarding the amount of change wrought in actual legal practice in New Mexico. While the topic is beyond the scope of this study, a few general observations are in order. Some scholars view the Mexican period as a time of increased intrusion on communal lands and a general deterioration of civil rights, but see little *de facto* change in dealing with Indian affairs.[50] Others stress that the altered legal status of Indians during the Mexican period facilitated Hispanic encroachment "through the legal sale of Pueblo lands as well as through the illegal actions of squatters."[51]

Encroachment undoubtedly occurred, but if natives assumed equal status during this period, there was never a successful or concerted effort in New Mexico to break up communal landholdings of the various Pueblo groups. Documentation from throughout the Mexican regime demonstrates that native communities continued to act as corporate units in defending their land rights, and not as individual landowners.[52] Demographic changes in the nineteenth century may have had as much to do with increased pressure on Indian lands as did perceptions of the natives' legal status. But on the whole, and for a variety of reasons, the Pueblos were less successful in retaining their land base during the Mexican and early American periods.

50. Jenkins, "The Baltasar Baca 'Grant'," pp. 60–61; Herbert O. Brayer, *Pueblo Indian Land Grants of the "Rio Abajo," New Mexico* (Albuquerque: University of New Mexico Press, 1939), pp. 19, 71, passim.
51. G. Emlen Hall and David J. Weber, "Mexican Liberals and the Pueblo Indians, 1821–1829," *New Mexico Historical Review* 59 (January 1984):19–22, quote on p. 20.
52. SANM I:1373, Pueblo de Laguna v. Cebolleta, 28 August 1827; and SANM I:1381, Pueblo of Isleta v. Juan Otero, 27 March 1845, are just two examples.

Chapter 5

The lessons in Hispanic jurisprudence were not forgotten overnight, and, at least in the early years of Mexican rule, Indians continued to appeal to authorities on the basis of their past experience. In 1822, for example, the pueblo of San Juan complained about the treatment received from their priest, Fray Mariano Sánchez Vergara (the ex-protector's brother), and asked for an outside protector. The natives claimed that Ignacio Sánchez Vergara did not protect them adequately, and that since Felipe Sandoval had died they had been "as orphans because we do not understand Castilian well, and because our understanding [of legal matters] is not as complete as that of the vecinos." Not only had the San Juan people alluded to a nonexistent office, but, despite the professed equality offered by the new Mexican nation, they made their petition on the basis of the special minority status that had held sway under Spanish rule.[53] While the office did not exist under the new government, Indians did resort to other tactics that they had learned as Spanish subjects. Frequently, for example, the natives secured the services of a procurador, who functioned as their legal representative in much the same way as had the protector.[54]

Still, official protection and special legal status were missing under Mexican rule. Especially after the mid-1830s, when local figures gained control of the territorial govern-

53. MANM r. 1, fr. 1184, Petition of Indians of San Juan, [Chihuahua], 1 January 1822.
54. One scholar has asserted that the protector survived past the Spanish period, and served as the natives' representative under the new government. See Frances Leon Swadesh, *Los Primeros Pobladores: Hispanic Americans of the Ute Frontier* (Notre Dame, Ind.: University of Notre Dame Press, 1974), p. 53. She perhaps confuses the procurador acting on behalf of a specific Indian pueblo with the protector de indios of the Spanish era.

ment, institutions and impartial officials who might defend Indian interests were lacking in New Mexico. Undoubtedly, the absence of the protector de indios served to further hinder the Indians' ability to secure legal redress.

The nineteenth century was, at once, a time of continuity and change in the history of Indian involvement with Hispanic jurisprudence. The familiarity with the system, which they had acquired in the eighteenth century, carried over into the next century. Indeed, Pueblos appear to have been even more confident of their ability to further their ends by pursuing Spanish justice. Direct Indian action led both to the reestablishment of the office of protector de indios in New Mexico as well as to the successful maintenance of property rights in local and high-level litigation. Enlightenment ideas, on the other hand, brought about drastic changes for the native population of the Spanish colonies. Not only did their status as minors with special privilege change, leading to the dismantling of such offices as the protector, but, equally important, the whole colonial structure toppled.

Although the new nation of Mexico had no place for differential status within the framework of its political philosophy, New Mexicans appear to have made no particular effort to apply political theory to everyday practice. Officials of the Mexican territorial government generally recognized communal rights, and Indians continued to appeal to authorities in some of the same ways as they had under Spanish rule. Still, an important change had occurred. Without the professed ideal of special protection, and the vigilance of officials such as the protector, outsiders severely encroached upon the land base of the Pueblo Indians.

Conclusion:
New Mexico
in Perspective

James S. Calhoun, first Indian agent and civil governor of New Mexico Territory, was impressed with the consistency with which the Pueblo Indians sought recourse for grievances through legal channels. "Scarcely a day passes," he noted, "that complaints are not brought before me of Mexican oppressions—Two deputations [of Pueblos] are now here." Less enthralled at a later date, Calhoun related that he had "been excessively annoyed, for the last fifteen days, by complaints from these Indians."[1] For the natives, faced with increased encroachment during the Mexican period, the American regime represented the hope of a new sov-

---

1. Annie Heloise Abel, ed., *The Official Correspondence of James S. Calhoun* (Washington, D.C.: Government Printing Office, 1915), pp. 88, 293. Other early observations relative to the Pueblos' bent for litigation include John Gilmary Shea, *History of the Catholic Missions among the Indian Tribes of the United States, 1529–1854* (New York: Edward Dunigan and Brother, 1855), p. 84.

ereign that might more effectively uphold their property rights. Yet the phenomenon of seemingly endless Pueblo appeals to justice was not some miraculous overnight adaptation to Anglo law. It was, instead, the product of their long experience with Hispanic jurisprudence.

As a component of the Spanish legal system in colonial New Mexico, the protector de indios was a figure of considerable importance. Although his functions varied slightly from his counterparts elsewhere in the empire, the similarities outweigh the differences.[2] No doubt the limited power of the protector as an agent of enforcement reflects the crown's fateful decision in the sixteenth century to make the office that of a legal representative. This role, however, proved highly valuable to Indians throughout the colonies.

The most important duty of the protector was to "aid and defend" the natives. This rather nebulous obligation could be satisfied in a variety of ways. Defense of the Indians took place primarily in the courtroom, but the protector was also to aid them "extrajudicially." Other duties included those of seeing to the indoctrination of the Indians in the Christian faith and of sending a report on the state of Indian affairs to the viceroy for eventual transmission to the Royal Council of the Indies. Protectors also had the responsibility of upholding native land rights and of nullifying any *composiciones de tierras* (settlements by fee of land titles) for tracts that Spaniards might have acquired contrary to royal law.[3] Later cédulas required the protector to guard against blacks, *mulatos*, Spaniards, and mestizos living in Indian

---

2. Most regulations pertaining to the protector are located in the *Recopilación de Leyes de Los Reynos de Las Indias* (Madrid: Julián de Paredes, 1681; facsimile reprint, Madrid: Ediciones Cultura Hispánica, 1973), tít. 6, lib. 6.

3. *Recopilación*, l. 17, tít. 12, lib. 4.

settlements, and to report any abusive working conditions to which the natives might be subjected. Like many other government officials, the protector could not trade with the natives.[4] A protector had to be of "competent age" and exercise his duties in a precise and "Christian-like manner." Although mestizos officially were barred from office, this provision was not universally enforced. Finally, the protector could not be removed from the position except with legitimate cause, and only after an investigation by the regional audiencia.

As far as the Indians were concerned, their sole obligation was to pay an annual assessment of one-half a *real* per person to cover legal expenses. This assessment, the *medio real*, paid not only for the protector, but for a number of other officials and services related to legal proceedings. Woodrow Borah has characterized the medio real as an early form of legal insurance.[5] In New Mexico, where Indians never paid this assessment, they still took advantage of Spanish legal machinery.[6]

On the far northern frontier, the protector clearly did not represent his charges in every court case. Even when this official existed in New Mexico, he took part in only a

---

4. Antonio Muro Orejón, *Cedulario Americano del Siglo XVIII*, tomo 1 (Sevilla: Escuela de Estudios Hispano-Americanos de Sevilla, 1956–1969), pp. 143–44, 507–9; tomo 2, pp. 564–65.

5. Woodrow Borah, *Justice by Insurance: The General Indian Court of Colonial Mexico and the Legal Aides of the Half-Real* (Berkeley: University of California Press, 1983), p. 5, passim.

6. See SANM II:420, "Residencia Dada Por el señor Dn Gerbasio Cruzat y Góngora . . . Resevida Por Dn Juan Joseph Brizeño y Súñiga . . . ," 26 August 1737. At this time, according to both Spaniards and Indians, the natives did not pay the medio real or any other form of regular tribute in New Mexico. This exemption appears to have been the case throughout the period of Spanish rule after 1680.

portion of the total number of cases involving Indians. While they often sought different channels through which to pursue Spanish justice, such as the governor, alcalde, or mission priest, Pueblos preferred to make use of the protector as their spokesman in defending their land claims. Extrajudicially, the protector seems to have played a minor role in New Mexico. Since his instructions on this point were vague, one may assume that extrajudicial help meant lodging protests against Spanish mistreatment of Indians. In colonial Potosí, for example, the duties of the local protector consisted primarily of maintaining prescribed working conditions for Indian laborers.[7] In a similar vein, Silvio Zavala cites numerous instances in which protectors throughout Peru actively sought to curb the colonists' disregard for legislation pertaining to labor regulations.[8] Examples of protectors in other regions acting against encomenderos who overworked or failed to indoctrinate Indians under their care indicate that extrajudicial watchfulness was an important duty of the position.[9] Only the actions of Antonio González in the seventeenth century are comparable, but he probably occupied the position only for the residencia of López de Mendizábal and did not exert constant pressure on Spanish colonists and officials.

7. Peter J. Bakewell, *Miners of the Red Mountain: Indian Labor in Potosí, 1545–1650* (Albuquerque: University of New Mexico Press, 1984), pp. 167–68.

8. Silvio Zavala, *El Servicio Personal de los Indios en el Perú* (México: El Colegio de México, 1980), tomo 3, passim; see especially pp. 106–8 concerning Vitorián de Villava who worked tirelessly to regularize the labor code.

9. Néstor Meza Villalobos, *Historia de la Política Indígena del Estado Español en América* (Santiago: Ediciones de la Universidad de Chile, 1976), pp. 990–92; José María Ots Capdequí, *Las Instituciones del Nuevo Reino de Granada al Tiempo de Independencia* (Madrid: Consejo Superior de Investigaciones Científicas, Instituto Gonzalo Fernández de Oviedo, 1958), pp. 239–77.

Conclusion

Christian indoctrination of the Indians in New Mexico was of minor concern to the protectors. Ignacio Sánchez Vergara alone sent the required report on the state of spiritual affairs to the audiencia. Nor did the protector keep constant vigil to bar racial outsiders from native villages. On the other hand, all of the known protectores de indios in New Mexico fit the prescription of being "Spanish." Designations such as these, especially on the frontier, were more often cultural than racial; certainly none of the New Mexico protectors were considered "mestizo." Whether they fulfilled their duties in a "Christian-like manner" is perhaps a question that has no objective answer.

Protectors in the nineteenth century held the office for life, but earlier, life tenure was not characteristic of New Mexico. Seventeenth- and eighteenth-century protectors usually performed the duties of office for only a few years. There was no known investigation by the audiencia that caused these men to lose their titles of office. In all probability, officials in New Mexico took lightly, or were unaware of, the requirement of life tenure.

Protectores de indios elsewhere, particularly in the audiencias, quite often were men with considerable legal training. Those in New Mexico had no such formal preparation. Nevertheless, although education on the frontier was an exception, the caliber of those who served as protectors undoubtedly was above average. An even more striking difference for protectorship in New Mexico was its uneven application. Indeed, for nearly 100 years, from 1717 to 1810, the office lay vacant.

Still, these variations appear to have been of minor consequence. While shortcomings and inconsistencies in the application of office are evident, the function and underlying philosophy of the protector de indios was crucial for the Indians of New Mexico. To be sure, legal protection did not depend solely upon the presence of this official, and other channels were available to Indians. But the protectorship proved to be an effective vehicle by which the Pueblos defended their land titles. Moreover, the impact of colonial legal practice is still felt today. Litigious activity of Pueblo groups during the Spanish period established precedents that are important to the maintenance of their present-day territorial integrity. The legal culture of colonial New Mexico provided Pueblo Indians with their first experience at active participation in a nonindigenous system of law. Within that system, the protector de indios often played a key role.

Sources

Archival Collections

Archives of the Archdiocese of Santa Fe, Albuquerque,
  New Mexico.
Archivo General de Indias, Seville, Spain:
  Contaduría
  Guadalajara
  México
  Patronato
Archivo General de la Nación, México, D.F., Mexico:
  Historia
  Inquisición
  Provincias Internas
  Tierras
Archivo de Hidalgo de Parral, Chihuahua, Mexico.
Archivo Histórico Nacional, Madrid, Spain:
  Diversos
  Reales Cédulas

Sources

Biblioteca del Estado de Jalisco, Guadalajara, Jal., Mexico:
   Archivo de la Real Audiencia de Guadalajara
Biblioteca Nacional, Madrid, Spain:
   Manuscritos
Biblioteca Nacional, México, D.F., Mexico.
New Mexico State Archives and Records Center, Santa Fe,
   New Mexico:
   Mexican Archives of New Mexico
   Spanish Archives of New Mexico
   Records of U.S. Surveyor General
University of New Mexico General Library, Special Collections, Albuquerque, New Mexico.

Printed Documents

Abel, Annie Heloise, ed. *The Official Correspondence of James S. Calhoun.* Washington, D.C.: Government Printing Office, 1915.
Cedulario de las Provincias de Santa Marta y Cartagena de Indias. Madrid: Librería General de Victoriano Suárez, 1913.
Colección de Documentos Inéditos de Ultramar. 25 vols. Madrid: 1885–1932.
Colección de Documentos Inéditos para la Historia de España. 113 vols. Madrid: 1842–1895.
Colección de Documentos Inéditos Relativos al Descubrimiento, Conquista y Colonización de las Posesiones en América y Oceanía. 42 vols. Madrid: 1864–1884.
Encinas, Diego de. *Cedulario Indiano.* 4 vols. Madrid: Imprenta Real, 1596. Facsimile reprint. Madrid: Ediciones Cultura Hispánica, 1945–1946.
Levillier, Roberto. *Gobernantes del Perú: Cartas y Papeles,*

Sources

Siglo XVI. Madrid: Biblioteca del Congreso Argentino, 1925.

Muro Orejón, Antonio. *Cedulario Americano del Siglo XVIII.* 2 vols. Sevilla: Escuela de Estudios Hispano-Americanos de Sevilla, 1956–1969.

Novísima Recopilación de las Leyes de España. Madrid: 1805. Facsimile reprint. Madrid: Boletín Oficial del Estado, 1976.

Ortega Ricaurte, Enrique. *Acuerdos de la Real Audiencia del Nuevo Reino de Granada.* Bogotá: Archivo Nacional de Colombia, 1948.

Otte, Enrique. *Cédulas Reales Relativas a Venezuela, 1500–1550.* Caracas: Fundación John Boulton y La Fundación Eugenio Mendoza, 1963.

Puga, Vasco de. *Provisiones, Cédulas, Instrucciones Para el Gobierno de la Nueva España.* México: Pedro Ocharte, 1563. Facsimile reprint. Madrid: Ediciones Cultura Hispánica, 1945.

Recopilación de Leyes de Los Reynos de Las Indias. 4 vols. Madrid: Julián de Paredes, 1681. Facsimile reprint. Madrid: Ediciones Cultura Hispánica, 1973.

Las Siete Partidas del Sabio Rey don Alonso el nono. 3 vols. Salamanca: Andrea de Portonaris, 1555. Facsimile reprint. Madrid: Boletín Oficial del Estado, 1974.

Solórzano Pereira, Juan de. *Política Indiana.* Madrid: 1647. Reprint. Madrid and Buenos Aires: Compañía Ibero-Americana de Publicaciones, S.A., 1930.

Books and Articles

Bakewell, Peter J. *Miners of the Red Mountain: Indian Labor in Potosí, 1545–1650.* Albuquerque: University of New Mexico Press, 1984.

Sources

——. *Silver Mining and Society in Colonial Mexico: Zacatecas, 1546–1700.* Cambridge: Cambridge University Press, 1971.

Bayle, Constantino. *El Protector de Indios.* Sevilla: Escuela de Estudios Hispano-Americanos de la Universidad de Sevilla, 1945.

Bloom, Lansing B. "The Vargas Encomienda." *New Mexico Historical Review* 14 (October 1939):366–417.

——, transcriber. "Ynstrucción a Peralta por Vi-Rey." *New Mexico Historical Review* 4 (April 1929):178–87.

Borah, Woodrow. *Justice by Insurance: The General Indian Court of Colonial Mexico and the Legal Aides of the Half-Real.* Berkeley: University of California Press, 1983.

Brayer, Herbert O. *Pueblo Indian Land Grants of the "Rio Abajo," New Mexico.* Albuquerque: University of New Mexico Press, 1939.

Burkholder, Mark A. *Politics of a Colonial Career: José Baquíjano and the Audiencia of Lima.* Albuquerque: University of New Mexico Press, 1980.

Caso, Alfonso et al. *Métodos y Resultados de la Política Indigenista en México.* México: Instituto Nacional Indigenista, 1954.

Céspedes del Castillo, Guillermo. "La Visita como Institución Indiana." *Anuario de Estudios Americanos* 3 (1946):984–1025.

Chamberlain, R. S. "Castilian Backgrounds of the Repartimiento-Encomienda." *Contributions to American Anthropology and History* 25 (June 1939):19–66.

Chavez, Angelico. *Archives of the Archdiocese of Santa Fe, 1678–1900.* Washington, D.C.: Academy of Franciscan History, 1957.

——. "Genízaros." In Alfonso Ortiz, ed., *Handbook of*

Sources

North American Indians: The Southwest. Vol. 9. Washington, D.C.: Smithsonian Institution, 1979.

———. *Origins of New Mexico Families.* Santa Fe: Historical Society of New Mexico, 1954.

Chevalier, François. *Land and Society in Colonial Mexico: The Great Hacienda.* Translated by Alvin Eustis. Edited by Lesley Byrd Simpson. Berkeley and Los Angeles: University of California Press, 1963.

Cordell, Linda S. "Prehistory: Eastern Anasazi." In Alfonso Ortiz, ed., *Handbook of North American Indians: The Southwest.* Vol. 9. Washington, D.C.: Smithsonian Institution, 1979.

Díaz, José Simón. *Fuentes para la Historia de Madrid y su Provincia.* Madrid: Instituto de Estudios Madrileños, 1964.

Dozier, Edward P. *The Pueblo Indians of North America.* New York: Holt, Rinehart and Winston, 1970.

Elliot, J. H. *Imperial Spain, 1469–1716.* New York: New American Library, 1966.

Espinosa, J. Manuel. *Crusaders of the Rio Grande: The Story of Don Diego de Vargas and the Reconquest and Refounding of New Mexico.* Chicago: Institute of Jesuit History, 1942.

———, trans., with introduction and notes. *The First Expedition of Vargas into New Mexico, 1692.* Albuquerque: University of New Mexico Press, 1940.

Eugenio Martínez, María Ángeles. *Tributo y Trabajo del Indio en Nueva Granada.* Sevilla: Escuela de Estudios Hispano-Americanos de Sevilla, 1977.

Fernández-Arroyo y Cabeza de Vaca, Manuela, and Jesús Villalmanzo Cameno. *Catálogo de la Serie de Real Justicia.* Madrid: Servicio de Publicaciones del Ministerio de Educación y Ciencias, 1976.

Sources

Foote, Cheryl J., and Sandra K. Schackel. "Indian Women of New Mexico, 1535–1680." In Darlis A. Miller and Joan Jensen, ed., *New Mexico Women*. Albuquerque: University of New Mexico Press, 1986.

Forbes, Jack D. *Apache, Navaho and Spaniard*. Norman: University of Oklahoma Press, 1960.

García-Gallo, Concepción. *Las Notas a la Recopilación de Leyes de Indias, de Salas, Martínez de Rozas y Boix*. Madrid: Ediciones Cultura Hispánica del Centro Iberoamericano de Cooperación, 1979.

García Icazbalceta, Joaquín. *Don Fray Juan de Zumárraga, Primer Obispo y Arzobispo de México*. México: Editorial Porrúa, S.A., 1947.

Gibson, Charles. *Tlaxcala in the Sixteenth Century*. Stanford, Calif.: Stanford University Press, 1967.

Góngora, Mario. *Studies in the Colonial History of Spanish America*. Cambridge: Cambridge University Press, 1975.

Hall, G. Emlen. *Four Leagues of Pecos: A Legal History of the Pecos Grant, 1800–1933*. Albuquerque: University of New Mexico Press, 1984.

———, and David J. Weber. "Mexican Liberals and the Pueblo Indians, 1821–1829." *New Mexico Historical Review* 59 (January 1984):5–32.

Hammond, George P., and Agapito Rey. *Don Juan de Oñate: Colonizer of New Mexico, 1595–1628*. 2 vols. Albuquerque: University of New Mexico Press, 1953.

———, ed. and trans. *Narratives of the Coronado Expedition, 1540–1542*. Albuquerque: University of New Mexico Press, 1940.

———. *The Rediscovery of New Mexico, 1580–1594: The Explorations of Chamuscado, Espejo, Castaño de Sosa, Morlete, and Leyva de Bonilla and Humaña*. Albuquerque: University of New Mexico Press, 1966.

Hanke, Lewis. *All Mankind Is One: A Study of the Disputation Between Bartolomé de Las Casas and Juan Ginés de Sepúlveda in 1550 on the Intellectual and Religious Capacity of American Indians.* DeKalb, Ill. Northern Illinois University Press, 1974.

———. *The Spanish Struggle for Justice in the Conquest of America.* Philadelphia: University of Pennsylvania Press, 1949.

———. *La Lucha por la Justicia en la Conquista de América.* Buenos Aires: Editorial Sudamericana, 1949.

Haring, C. H. *The Spanish Empire in America.* New York: Oxford University Press, 1947.

Hu-DeHart, Evelyn. *Missionaries, Miners and Indians: Spanish Contact with the Yaqui Nation of Northwestern New Spain, 1533–1820.* Tucson: University of Arizona Press, 1981.

Jaenen, Cornelius J. *Friend and Foe: Aspects of French-Amerindian Cultural Contact in the Sixteenth and Seventeenth Centuries.* New York: Columbia University Press, 1976.

Jenkins, Myra Ellen. "The Baltasar Baca 'Grant': History of an Encroachment." *El Palacio* 68 (Spring and Summer 1961):47–64, 87–105.

———. "Spanish Land Grants in the Tewa Area." *New Mexico Historical Review* 47 (April 1972):113–134.

———. "Taos Pueblo and Its Neighbors, 1540–1847." *New Mexico Historical Review* 41 (April 1966):85–114.

Jones, Oakah L. *Pueblo Warriors and Spanish Conquest.* Norman: University of Oklahoma Press, 1966.

Juan y Santacilia, Jorge, and Antonio de Ulloa. *Discourse and Political Reflections on the Kingdom of Peru.* Edited and introduction by John J. TePaske. Translated by John J. TePaske and Bessie A. Clement. Norman: University of Oklahoma Press, 1978.

Kagan, Richard L. *Lawsuits and Litigants in Castile: 1500–1700.* Chapel Hill: University of North Carolina Press, 1981.

Kelly, Henry W. *Franciscan Missions of New Mexico, 1740–1760.* Albuquerque: University of New Mexico Press, 1941.

Kessell, John L. "Diego Romero, the Plains Apaches, and the Inquisition." *The American West* 15 (May–June 1978):12–16.

———. "Esteban Clemente: Precursor of the Revolt." *El Palacio* 84 (Winter 1980–81):16–17.

———. *Kiva, Cross, and Crown: The Pecos Indians and New Mexico, 1540–1840.* Washington, D.C.: National Park Service, 1979.

Lamar, Howard Roberts. *The Far Southwest, 1846–1912: A Territorial History.* New York: W. W. Norton and Company, 1970.

Las Casas, Bartolomé de. *Historia de las Indias.* México and Buenos Aires: Fondo de Cultura Económica, 1951. Edición de Agustín Millares Carlo y estudio preliminar de Lewis Hanke.

Levillier, Roberto. *Don Francisco de Toledo: Supremo Organizador del Perú: Su Vida, Su Obra (1515–1582).* Madrid: Espasa-Calpe, S.A., 1935.

Madden, Marie R. *Political Theory and Law in Medieval Spain.* New York: Fordham University Press, 1930.

Mariluz Urquijo, José María. *Ensayo Sobre los Juicios de Residencia Indianos.* Sevilla: Escuela de Estudios Hispano-Americanos de Sevilla, 1952.

Meza Villalobos, Néstor. *Historia de la Política Indígena del Estado Español en América.* Santiago: Ediciones de la Universidad de Chile, 1976.

Moorhead, Max L. *New Mexico's Royal Road: Trade and*

Sources

Travel on the Chihuahua Trail. Norman: University of Oklahoma Press, 1958.

Morales Padrón, Francisco. *Teoría y Leyes de la Conquista*. Madrid: Ediciones Cultura Hispánica del Centro Ibero-Americano de Cooperación, 1979.

Navarro García, Luis. *Don José de Gálvez y la Comandancia General de las Provincias Internas del Norte de la Nueva España*. Sevilla: Escuela de Estudios Hispano-Americanos de Sevilla, 1964.

Offner, Jerome A. *Law and Politics in Aztec Texcoco*. Cambridge: Cambridge University Press, 1984.

Ortiz, Alfonso, ed. *Handbook of North American Indians: The Southwest*. Vol. 9. Washington, D.C.: Smithsonian Institution, 1979.

————. "Popay's Leadership: A Pueblo Perspective." *El Palacio* 86 (Winter 1980–81):18–22.

Ots Capdequí, José María. *Historia del Derecho Español en América y del Derecho Indiano*. Madrid: Aguilar, 1969.

————. *Las Instituciones del Nuevo Reino de Granada al Tiempo de Independencia*. Madrid: Consejo Superior de Investigaciones Científicas, Instituto Gonzalo Fernández de Oviedo, 1958.

Parry, J. H. *The Spanish Theory of Empire in the Sixteenth Century*. New York: Octagon Books, 1974.

Phelan, John Leddy. *The Millennial Kingdom of the Franciscans in the New World*. 2d ed. Berkeley and Los Angeles: University of California Press, 1970.

Powell, Philip Wayne. *Mexico's Miguel Caldera: The Taming of America's First Frontier, 1548–1597*. Tucson: University of Arizona Press, 1977.

————. *Soldiers, Indians and Silver: The Northward Advance of New Spain, 1550–1600*. Berkeley and Los Angeles: University of California Press, 1952.

Sources

Riley, Carroll J. *The Frontier People: The Greater Southwest in the Protohistoric Period.* Carbondale, Ill.: Center for Archaeological Investigations, Southern Illinois University at Carbondale, 1982.

Santamaría, Francisco J. *Diccionario General de Americanismos.* 3 vols. México: Editorial Pedro Robredo, 1942.

Scholes, France V. "Church and State in New Mexico." *New Mexico Historical Review* 11 (January 1936):9–76.

————. "Civil Government and Society in New Mexico in the Seventeenth Century." *New Mexico Historical Review* 10 (April 1935):71–111.

————. *Troublous Times in New Mexico, 1659–1670.* Albuquerque: University of New Mexico Press, 1942.

Schroeder, Albert H., and Dan S. Matson. *A Colony on the Move: Gaspar Castaño de Sosa's Journal, 1590–1591.* Santa Fe: School of American Research, 1965.

Shea, John Gilmary. *History of the Catholic Missions among the Indian Tribes of the United States, 1529–1854.* New York: Edward Dunigan and Brother, 1855.

Simmons, Marc. *Spanish Government in New Mexico.* Albuquerque: University of New Mexico Press, 1968.

Simpson, Lesley Byrd. *The Encomienda in New Spain: The Beginning of Spanish Mexico.* Berkeley and Los Angeles: University of California Press, 1966.

Spicer, Edward H. *Cycles of Conquest: The Impact of Spain, Mexico, and the United States on the Indians of the Southwest, 1533–1960.* Tucson: University of Arizona Press, 1962.

Stern, Steve J. *Peru's Indian Peoples and the Challenge of Spanish Conquest: Huamanga to 1640.* Madison: University of Wisconsin Press, 1982.

Swadesh, Frances Leon. *Los Primeros Pobladores: Hispanic*

Americans of the Ute Frontier. Notre Dame, Ind.: University of Notre Dame Press, 1974.

Taylor, William B. *Drinking, Homicide and Rebellion in Colonial Mexican Villages*. Stanford, Calif.: Stanford University Press, 1979.

———. *Landlord and Peasant in Colonial Oaxaca*. Stanford, Calif.: Stanford University Press, 1972.

Twitchell, Ralph Emerson. *The Leading Facts of New Mexican History*. 5 vols. Cedar Rapids, Iowa: Torch Press, 1911–17.

———. *The Spanish Archives of New Mexico*. 2 vols. Cedar Rapids, Iowa: Torch Press, 1914.

Vance, John Thomas. *The Background of Hispanic-American Law*. Washington, D.C.: Catholic University of America, 1937.

Vaughan, Alden T. *New England Frontier: Puritans and Indians, 1620–1675*. Rev. ed. New York and London: W. W. Norton and Company, 1979.

Wagner, Henry Raup, with the collaboration of Helen Rand Parish. *The Life and Writings of Bartolomé de las Casas*. Albuquerque: University of New Mexico Press, 1967.

Washburn, Wilcomb E. *Red Man's Land/White Man's Law: A Study of the Past and Present Status of the American Indian*. New York: Charles Scribner's Sons, 1971.

West, Robert C. *The Mining Community in Northern New Spain: The Parral Mining District*. Berkeley and Los Angeles: University of California Press, 1949.

Zavala, Silvio. *La Encomienda Indiana*. Segunda edición. México: Editorial Porrúa, S.A., 1973.

———. *El Servicio Personal de los Indios en el Perú*. 3 vols. México: El Colegio de México, 1980.

Index

Index

Index

Index